IN OUR MINDS
THERE IS
AWARENESS
OF PERFECTION.

—AGNES MARTIN

IN PURSUIT OF *perfection*

TIMOTHY ROBERT RODGERS

IN PURSUIT OF PERFECTION

THE ART OF AGNES MARTIN, MARIA MARTINEZ AND FLORENCE PIERCE

With essays by Marsha C. Bol, Lucy R. Lippard and Timothy Robert Rodgers

Museum of Fine Arts, Santa Fe, a division of the Department of Cultural Affairs

Distributed by the Museum of New Mexico Press and the Museum of Fine Arts

In Pursuit of Perfection: The Art of Agnes Martin, Maria Martinez and Florence Pierce is published in conjunction with the exhibition organized by Timothy Robert Rodgers for the Museum of Fine Arts, Santa Fe, a division of the Department of Cultural Affairs, 8 October 2004–23 January 2005.

Catalogue Design: David Mendez
Editor: Laura Addison
Exhibition Design: Susan Hyde-Holmes and John Tinker
Photographer: Blair Clark

ISBN 0-9675106-8-6
For inquiries or ordering information:
Museum of Fine Arts, P. O. Box 2087, Santa Fe, New Mexico 87504-2087
or Museum of New Mexico Press, 725 Camino Lejo, P. O. Box 2087, Santa Fe, New Mexico 87504-2087.
Phone 800-249-7737, fax 800-622-8667, website www.mnmpress.org

CONTENTS

Marsha C. Bol, Ph.D.
Director, Museum of Fine Arts, Santa Fe

FOREWORD

WHEN THE MUSEUM OF FINE ARTS OPENED IN 1917, ART BY NATIVE AMERICANS WAS PRESENTED ALONGSIDE THE WORK DONE BY ARTISTS TRAINED IN THE MODERN STYLES OF THE DAY. ALTHOUGH THESE ART FORMS AROSE OUT OF VERY DIFFERENT CULTURES and their respective concerns, the visual similarities linked the work in ways that the founders of the museum believed to be enlightening and visually informative. The Museum of Fine Arts seeks to revive the tradition of combining art of different times and cultures to provoke the eye and mind of the viewer.

In the exhibition *In Pursuit of Perfection: The Art of Agnes Martin, Maria Martinez and Florence Pierce*, Chief Curator Tim Rodgers brings together three of New Mexico's most acclaimed artists. Each renowned in her own right, these artists have never had their work presented together in an exhibition. When viewed, this stunning show will cause all to question why this has been so. How do artists, especially those who at one time lived only miles apart, come to exist in art worlds light years apart? How much has been gained and lost by the categories that both define and delimit this art?

It has been exciting for me as the director of the Museum of Fine Arts and as a scholar of Native American art to participate in the creation of this exhibition. I remember well Tim returning from a visit to Florence Pierce's studio and proposing an exhibition of art by Martinez, Martin and Pierce. He had seen in Pierce's home how she displayed Native American pottery, mainly gifts from artists she knew and admired, side by side with her luminous poured-resin paintings. Although unexpected, the relationship between the pottery and the paintings seemed to him visually exciting. He added Martin to the mix and began to think about how these artists related to one another.

Tim needed to step outside of typical constructions of art history and think like the artist Pierce, whom he much admired. A week later, *In Pursuit of Perfection* came into being. Centering the show on a powerful concept like the pursuit of perfection allowed him to ask questions that, when answered, began to weave together these artists and their creations. At its best, this has been one of New Mexico's gifts to the world of art: a truly multicultural art, a hybrid that offers surprising linkages and intersections across time and cultures.

Many people have helped with the creation of this exhibition. Tim thanks all at the end of this catalogue, but I would like to thank in particular Governor Bill Richardson and First Lady Barbara Richardson. Their support has meant everything for the success of this show and the museum itself. Their sophisticated understanding and unwavering support of the arts of New Mexico have revitalized our museum and its patrons. I also want to recognize the remarkable generosity of former New Mexico Representative J. Paul Taylor. He gave his time and energy to help secure funding for this exhibition; moreover, his support for all the arts of our state has secured his place in the history of New Mexico art. Finally, to our chief curator, Dr. Rodgers, I offer both thanks and congratulations on a job well done.

PERFECTION

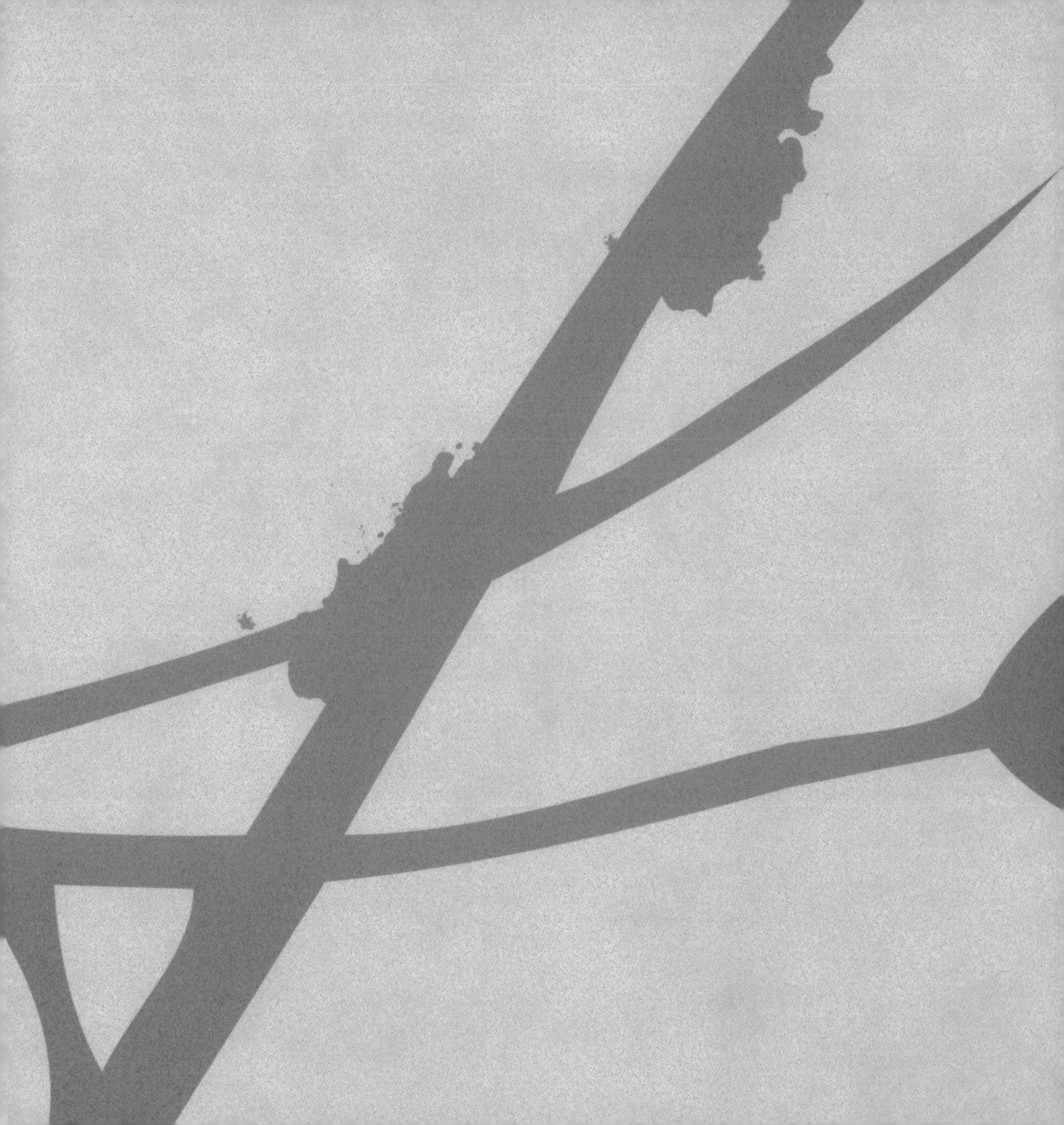

I HOPE THAT I HAVE MADE IT CLEAR THAT THE WORK IS ABOUT PERFECTION AS WE ARE AWARE OF IT IN OUR MINDS BUT THAT THE PAINTINGS ARE VERY FAR FROM BEING PERFECT—COMPLETELY REMOVED IN FACT—EVEN AS WE OURSELVES ARE. —AGNES MARTIN

Timothy Robert Rodgers, Ph.D.
Chief Curator, Museum of Fine Arts, Santa Fe

INTRODUCTION

THE MOST POWERFUL WORDS ARE THOSE MOST DIFFICULT TO DEFINE: HAPPINESS, FRIENDSHIP, PERFECTION. AGNES MARTIN'S CONTENTION THAT WE ALL KNOW WHAT PERFECTION IS IN OUR MINDS MIGHT BE TRUE, but, if surveyed, few would define perfection exactly the same. Perhaps because words such as these are bound by cultural constraints like time and place, education and class, it is impossible to create a universal definition.

Despite their amorphous nature, these terms are vested with enormous power by cultures that weave into their meaning concepts and behaviors deemed worthy of continual discussion, examination and negotiation. A consideration of perfection, for example, uncovers societal building blocks such as work, goals, standards, failure, power and spirituality. In this catalogue and exhibition, Marsha Bol, Lucy Lippard and I examine three different artists—Agnes Martin, Maria Martinez and Florence Pierce—and attempt to reveal how in the course of making their art these women use the concept of perfection to establish their aesthetic standards, pursue their artistic goals and explain their spiritual and cultural concerns. The conclusion of each essay is nearly the same: none of the artists achieved perfection and none claimed that they had. But in the pursuit of this elusive concept, the artists called upon their deepest beliefs to create their art.

What are those deep-seated beliefs that motivated these artists to establish extraordinarily high standards that they pursued at great personal cost? For each artist, the answer is different. Florence Pierce might point to the importance of light for her life and her art as a force that compelled her to repeat, refine and refine again her poured-resin paintings. In a recent series of paintings titled *Clouds*, she has created her most luminous work that literally seems to transcend the bounds of earth and exist somewhere between the light and the ground. Such earthly transcendence might be, for her, the path to perfection. Maria Martinez would answer these questions differently, in part because of the cultural position she held as a minority in a society dominated by non-Natives. For Martinez, spiritual and cultural concerns fused with Eurocentric expectations, compelling her to refine, continually, her shapes and their finish. The exactitude of her art fostered a buying public that allowed the artist to give back to her people. The ability to help others in need became the ultimate motive in her pursuit of perfection. Agnes Martin, who of the three has written and spoken most about perfection, has woven together her desire for happiness, love and serenity with her quest to achieve the impossible. Perfection, according to Martin, exists in those moments of great joy and peace, those moments that inspire her to create. The process of trying to recapture on canvas and paper fleeting positive emotions has become for Martin a means of staving off the less-than-perfect times of sorrow, fear and loneliness.

In bringing these artists and their work together in relation to a shared idea, I have tried to move outside of some of the ways in which their art is typically presented. Martin has strenuously objected to having her work associated with the Minimalists. Martinez's art has been bound by her time and ethnicity. Pierce's work has failed to be integrated into typical art categories and exists only on the margins of mainstream art history. But art history and its categories often function as much to obfuscate art as to clarify it. What artists recognize is that they can connect with art produced across time and cultures as much as with something created in their own time and place. Art's eternal presence, its everlasting life, should not be buried in coffins of categories that create neat, linear histories. I would like to think that I am participating in the freeing of these artists and their work from such limitations. I know this exhibit has certainly freed my thinking about themes for art exhibitions. Wouldn't the art of Maria Martinez, Ad Reinhardt and Kara Walker make a stunning exhibition about the significance of black?

BEAUTY...IS NOT
IN THE EYE
IT IS IN THE MIND.

—AGNES MARTIN

Timothy Robert Rodgers

AGNES MARTIN
PORTRAIT OF A MIND

"AGNES MARTIN'S WORK . . . IS MYSTERIOUSLY MAGNETIC, YET THERE IS SO LITTLE ON WHICH TO GET ONE'S FOOTING, THAT THE PAINTINGS SEEM TO DEFY ARTICULATION AND OUR DESIRE TO ASSIGN MEANING TO THEM."[1]

In this confession from his 2002 catalogue essay "Agnes Martin—The Music of the Spheres," Ned Rifkin echoes the frustrations of many writers. Most of them, like Rifkin, readily acknowledge the paintings' evocative qualities, commonly referred to as lyrical, spiritual and sublime. Once articulated, however, the writers have been unwilling or unable to use their responses to advance possible interpretations of the work. "Exceedingly superficial and repetitive literature on Agnes Martin" has been the result, according to scholar Rosalind Krauss.[2] Considering Martin's status in the world of art, this is both surprising and intriguing.

Martin certainly deserves some of the blame—or credit—for this situation. Her post-1960s paintings, comprised mainly of horizontal lines, grids and diluted colors on square canvases, fit visually within the art-history category Minimalism. As a matter of fact, galleries and museums to this day present Martin's work most often in relation to that of Minimalist artists Donald Judd, Carl Andre and Sol LeWitt. Martin denies, with some justification, this connection. She considers herself an Abstract Expressionist. For the artist, this term means exactly what it implies: an artist who creates abstract works that express emotions. According to the painter, her non-referential art originates from personal inspirations, "visions of perfection," and conveys "subtle moments of happiness," love and/or innocence. Martin's self-labeling as an Abstract Expressionist has a certain logic that stands contrary to the typical Minimalist who attempts to make art impersonally and mechanically to underscore its intellectualism. But, in reality, art writers have seldom analyzed Abstract Expressionist works in light of emotions because of the dominance of a type of art criticism codified as formalism.

Inspired by the writings of Clement Greenberg in the 1950s and Michael Fried in the 1960s, formalism stressed the ways in which the overall shape, colors, surfaces and internal forms related to one another. Formalists, as they came to be called, granted art (most particularly Abstract Expressionist paintings) a purity of conception and execution that denied external influences. Believers in formalism could, therefore, "read" paintings without any knowledge of the artist's psychology or culture. This supposedly freed art criticism and art history from their earlier reliance on scientific theories, psychological speculations, historical facts and anthropological surveys. Because Clement Greenberg refined his theories in his writings on, and advocacy for, the Abstract Expressionists, these artists' work has largely been proscribed by formalist analysis. For Martin's work to fit neatly into the category of Abstract Expressionism as defined by formalism, her paintings would need to be viewed mainly in terms of forms, lines and shapes. Martin's insistence in her writings and lectures that her paintings refer to an inner emotional world stymies those who might attempt to advance a purely formalist interpretation. Moreover, her quiet, repetitive paintings have limited visual similarities to the work of Abstract Expressionists such as Willem de Kooning or Jackson Pollock.

Critics might have sidestepped the issue of taxonomy and more aggressively pursued a psychoanalytical approach to Martin's work had she not claimed, like many Western artists of the twentieth century, that her art must simply be experienced, and that the encounter should remain both wordless and silent. In an attempt to circumvent this problem, writers such as Barbara Haskell have tried to link Martin's insistence on paraverbal inspiration for her art to her exposure to Taoism and Zen during her studies at Columbia University.[3] Although historically accurate, and certainly noteworthy, documenting Martin's partial embrace of Eastern philosophies only underscores her rejection of interpretation and intellectual analysis. For example, Martin believes that there is a wide range of emotional responses to art that cannot be put into words.[4] Thus, citing her interest in Eastern philosophies further undermines the possibility of analytic interpretation of her work.

Finally, the post-1970s paintings also seem to limit interpretation. The ubiquitous horizontal bands, the slightly imperfect graphite "outlines," the pale, diluted acrylic colors washed onto the square canvases—all offer little obvious information with which to construct interpretations. For these reasons, many writers have only presented their general emotional responses to and observations of Martin's work. And, in so doing, they have reinforced the interpretive roadblocks Martin has consciously and unconsciously established for her work. Martin's reasons for erecting these roadblocks, however, are more complex than an attempt either to subvert criticism and categorization or to show allegiance to Eastern thought. Investigating why she blocks the interpretive process will yield, I believe, an approach to understanding both the artist and her work.

At its core, the desire to pursue interpretations beyond the artist's stated intentions, to give words to visual experience, is, simply, the need of one curious mind to engage another via the intermediary of art. The critic and historian Donald Kuspit wrote that "art was essentially relational," and involved "the artist and the seriously engaged receiver of the art, who is equally creative. Each needs the other to fulfill or complete his identity and destiny. Without this 'dialectical couple,' . . . no art, no identity, no meaning."[5]

Martin intentionally undermines the formation of the "dialectical couple" because her paintings reflect, according to the artist, only her inner life, her moments of inspiration. She has contended that she creates them "with her back to the world"—rather like someone looking in a mirror.[6] The picture created in a mirror is a supposed duplicate of the object in front of it and cannot be widely misinterpreted as being something that it is not. And, seeing oneself in a mirror is a highly personal experience that is most fully understood by the individual. Martin believes that, like a mirror, her paintings re-present as accurately as possible her visions related to fleeting, subtle emotions. An observer of her abstractions, according to Martin, cannot claim to see references to fields, oceans or sky because the paintings represent her visions and nothing else. Thus, when the interviewer Joan Simon asked Martin whether her work made reference to textile art, particularly that of Lenore Tawney, the artist replied, "Oh, don't give me that." When Simon pursued the matter further, Martin contended that whoever said that was attempting to undercut her achievements.[7]

Although producing art only in reference to her inspirations certainly makes its meaning clear to Martin, the same cannot necessarily be said for her audience. Most viewers would have a hard time looking at her grids and understanding that they are, as she states, about innocence. Likewise, viewing her more recent stripe paintings and experiencing the feelings she wishes to elicit—love, happiness or purity—takes a leap of faith. Her stated inspirations, at face value, provide little material for interpretation. The broader idea that her paintings reflect moments of her inner life does, however, encourage examination of her inner life, her voices, the meaning of her reductive and repetitive language of abstraction and her obsessive need to express and control emotion.[8] These issues, so often alluded to by the artist and only cursorily examined by the critics, I will address in the following pages.

Martin hears voices, has inspirations. She will not specify where she believes her inspirations come from

other than to say that they are from her mind. In an odd exchange with Joan Simon, Martin described the situation thus:

> (Simon) How do you begin to work?
>
> (Martin) When I set out to do a painting, I ask for an inspiration. And I follow it.
>
> (Simon) Whom or what are you asking for inspiration?
>
> (Martin) My mind.
>
> (Simon) Does it sometimes not answer?[9]

Although sometimes she has to wait for weeks, even months, for her mind to answer, Martin believes she has been so inspired throughout her life. She is not the only person to make this claim; some religious individuals, for example, record being enlightened from a divine source. The artist's often repeated statement, however, that her inspirations spring from an unknown and unknowable part of her mind is unusual.

Martin's vehement rejection of any type of external influence—artistic or otherwise—in part explains her assertion. For Martin to claim to have been inspired by anyone, even God, would make her a follower not in touch with her true self. To explain her inspirations without citing an external source, Martin subdivided her mind so that at least part of it speaks to other parts. This dissociation allows Martin to deny, as she sometimes does, that she is the creator of her art. Such claims also help fulfill her desire to embody humility free of ego and influence.

As if to protect herself further from outside influences, Martin has physically isolated herself since the late 1960s. She has lived in very remote areas of New Mexico in extremely spartan environments, often without a telephone, television, electricity or running water. Even today, at the age of ninety-two, she allows herself few material goods and even fewer luxuries. Her world is circumscribed; recently she said that she spends her mornings painting and her afternoons thinking about the paintings.[10]

The mental and physical dissociations Martin advances as explanations for her inspirations and lack of influence parallel her recurring statements about perfection. Martin readily acknowledges that her work is "about perfection as we are aware of it in our minds but . . . the paintings are very far from being perfect."[11] Although far less unusual, Martin's clear division of her mental images from her created images underscores the bifurcations she creates in her life. These divisions are often of a specific type: on the one side, perfection, simplicity, humility and universality; and on the other, imperfection, irregularity, ego and individuality.

Conflicts and tensions marble Martin's life as a result of these divisions. Three such conflicts are readily apparent. First, creating hundreds of six-by-six-foot paintings with extremely reduced yet easily identifiable patterns, and then sending them yearly to New York to be shown at an internationally known gallery, requires a sense of self not associated with the humble, anonymous craftsperson. Second, New Mexico in the 1970s was not uncharted territory; establishing oneself even in the most remote parts meant you were following in the footsteps of legendary artists such as John Sloan, Robert Henri, John Marin and Georgia O'Keeffe, to name only a few. Third, claiming that

your ideas are inspirations solely self-derived undercuts the notion of training, learning and schooling. (Martin trained to be a teacher at one of the finest universities, Columbia, where she later pursued a master's degree in education. Afterwards, she sought a second master's degree in art from the University of New Mexico, where she eventually became a professor of art.)

Few artists possessing both Martin's intelligence and sincerity would continually voice such contradictions—especially in the face of the critical scrutiny the artist and her work have generated. "Prophet," "messiah" and "priest" are just some of the names the critics have ascribed to Martin (sometimes ironically, sometimes not) to justify her conflicting statements, actions and creations. Although to some degree Martin is consciously constructing what she believes to be an appropriate artist persona for the public, her behavior seems too extreme, her actions and words too consistent, not to be genuinely held. The mental tension that must result from holding such beliefs can, I believe, be seen in the works.

Considering that Martin has been painting for approximately fifty years, her work conveys a surprising tentativeness. The transparent horizontal stripes she has painted almost exclusively for the past thirty or more years seem, from a distance, fairly graphic and reasonably assured. However, upon closer inspection, the stripes fail to completely fill in the graphite outlines. Because she does not use any type of resists, she applies the color as close to the line as possible, freehand. A slight white separation exists between the graphite line and the color wash, like a conscientious child's coloring inside the lines. This white separation quivers in relation to the outline as Martin carefully, but not too skillfully, moves her paintbrush down the canvas. (Martin paints the horizontal stripes vertically so that the thin paint will run down the surface in the direction of the stripe. When finished, the works are then displayed horizontally.) Although she applies the watered-down acrylic paint with a light touch, the traces of the brush-mark never belie the years she has been painting. In other words, her workmanlike brush-marks never change much, they never become more or less proficient.

Similar to the colored stripes, the graphite lines that form the outlines of the stripes read from a distance as assured. Up close, however, they appear very different because the artist uses an eighteen-inch ruler to create her lines, and the slight overlaps and shifts in the ruler over a stretch of five or six feet make the line unsteady. She justifies this practice by noting that the "bounce" of the stretched canvas prevents her from using a longer measuring tool. Other more effective devices do exist, however, and Martin's continued use of the ruler needs to be understood as her desire to leave evident hand-made marks. Although her small drawings have fewer such distortions, the grids and stripes do show slight mishaps that occur, for example, when the ruler has not been placed exactly parallel to the line above it. Also, like the colored sections of the stripes, the graphite lines appear to waver, particularly on the large canvases, because Martin varies the pressure she applies to the pencil. Never overly dark, the graphite ranges from a whisper to a statement. Occasionally, the pencil bobbles across the textured surface leaving white skips. (Martin

uses just enough gesso on the canvas, two coats, to retain some of the surface texture.)

Because of her light application of the graphite and acrylic, Martin's paintings are often referred to as quiet, contemplative, even serene. I would agree that the paintings do on some level announce themselves humbly, however in other ways they can be rather strident. Since the 1970s, Martin has created paintings that are either five by five or six by six feet. The scale of the work is in relation to Martin's body; she switched to the five-foot size because the larger ones were becoming too difficult to maneuver in her advancing years. When first encountered, the paintings engulf and confront the viewer. Slightly (or not so slightly) larger than a person, the paintings do not overwhelm to the point of awe due to their scale, but instead present themselves as sumo wrestlers—human, yes; typical, no; intimidating, yes. Martin often conceives of her work in series, so, for example, the Whitney Museum of American Art's grouping *The Islands* (1979) consists of twelve six-by-six-foot canvases that the artist insists must be presented as one unit. At nearly one hundred running feet, the surfaces might seem subdued, but the scale of the work is not. Thus, the paintings, when examined closely, convey the contradictions apparent in Martin's life and writings: humble/egotistical, quiet/loud, repetitive/unique, insistent/demure, graphic/handmade, complex/simple.

Martin's drawings, unlike most of her paintings, are often rather small—about ten by ten inches. The small scale of the drawings allows the viewer to grasp them physically—literally to possess the work in their hands. As if to deny the viewer such power over her work, Martin often increases the volume of the drawings by darkening the lines and making them more precise. For the same reason, but by opposite means, Martin will sometimes lighten the lines and colors so that the drawings seem to disappear in your hands.

The tensions noted overall in the drawings' and paintings' surfaces play out again in Martin's signature form: the horizontal stripe. Martin has stated that for the past thirty or more years she has worked almost exclusively with the horizontal line. As the name implies, such a line typically divides a rectangular canvas in the manner of a horizon. The relationship between a rectangular canvas and the horizon line in Western cultures is so expected that viewers readily and comfortably accept the pairing. As a result, at first Martin's horizontal lines appear to have a placid demeanor. But, by using multiple lines on the same canvas, she quickly undercuts a connection to a horizon line. Moreover, the multiple horizontal lines placed on a square canvas divide it into an array of rectangular shapes that compete with the overall form. Martin has admitted (a confession she later attempted to retract) to creating this adversarial relationship in an attempt to undermine the dominance of the square.[12] She has not acknowledged the irresolvable tension it can create for the viewer.

Martin's paintings when viewed en masse or in series become even more disquieting. Canvas after canvas of horizontal lines drains the lines of their strength as subject matter (a stripe, a horizon line, a form, a divider) and, finally, they point toward an obsession. Because the works are so self-referential, by her own account, Martin's obsession is clearly with herself. For this reason, perhaps, Martin packs the simple stripes with broad significance. As noted earlier, the stripes are meant to convey subtle, but profound, emotions like love, happiness and joy. By repeating the horizontal lines Martin attempts to recapture the experience of these emotions. Although not as resonant as the actual experience, the lines apparently satisfy Martin's needs. But what drives these desires?

The art writer Holland Cotter attempted an answer to this question. He believes that Martin's "choice of calm over chaos, in her art and in her life has the force of a psychological imperative: a need to seek stable patterns in a world full of unpredictable change, to get beyond the disharmonies of embarrassment, hope, desire, loss, guilt and fear, to find a mechanism for serenity that is fine-tuned and ever-ready, allowing her to be reassured and thus productive."[13] Generally reticent on this subject, Martin did state in a recent documentary by Mary Lance, *With My Back to the World*, that she considers the horizontal lines as emotional divides: above the line exist positive emotions; below, negative.[14] Although I would be hesitant to interpret Martin's stripes so succinctly, both Cotter and the artist indicate that emotions and thoughts deemed negative motivate the artist as much as positive ones. In other words, Martin's obsessive need to *reproduce* happiness, for example, at a certain point begins to read as a personal failure to consistently *experience* happiness. Martin nearly states this in one of her attempts to explain "moments of perfection." During such moments she "suddenly becomes very happy" and she "wonders why life ever seemed troublesome." In an instant, the painter "sees the road ahead free from difficulties and we think that we will never lose it again. All this and a great deal more in barely a moment, and then it is gone."[15]

Failure to sustain happiness must foster for Martin ongoing fear, anxiety and desperation. Martin affirms this in a powerful description of her despair:

> Moments of helplessness are moments of blindness. One feels as though something terrible has happened without knowing what it is. One feels as though one is in the outer darkness or as though one has made some terrible error—a fatal error. Our great help that we leaned on in the dark has deserted us and we are in complete panic and we feel that we have got to have help. The panic of complete helplessness drives us to fantastic extremes. . . . [16]

The act of painting for Martin becomes the antidote, the anti-depressant that reassures the artist that happiness will be and can be re-experienced. And by ceaselessly painting she holds off the panic, the moments of helplessness as she clings to her remembered inspirations.

Martin would like to believe that the paintings that result from the tensions and struggles described bear no scars. She would like to believe that a sensitive viewer only experiences the subtle, positive emotions that she strives so adamantly to express. The depression, fear, anxiety, compulsions and darkness never gain expression because she has struggled so hard to subdue them. For art to have meaning for more than just the artist, however, viewers of art must be allowed to interpret the work for themselves. Without this freedom, art is not experienced, it is dictated.

What do I see when I view Martin's paintings? At first I am struck by their openness, their ethereal presence that vaporizes at a distance. Quiet, extraordinarily sensitive, fragile are my adjectives of choice. Rather quickly, however, their less obvious qualities rise to the surface: obsessive, tense and unsteady. The never-ending horizontal lines, the tension between the canvas and the internal forms, the on-going strife between the graphite lines and the washed colors, the quivering of the brush and pencil—all recall the difficult mental and emotional struggle undertaken to produce the work. With this in mind, I begin to empathize with the artist and her struggles and I think about what would drive someone to paint horizontal lines for thirty or more years. Something deeper than joy and happiness, something unresolved and perhaps irresolvable must be at the core. A conflict, a tension so fundamental that it requires the artist's full attention, demands almost all of her waking moments. This war must have, at its heart, life and death. Or, as Martin has said, "struggling from death into life."[17]

Sharing her personal battle takes immense courage and fortitude. The fact that Martin steps back from the interpretive process, and moves away from the complications her paintings present, can easily be forgiven because of what she offers. "The exploration of [the] mind and the adventures within the mind," Martin recommends to all and offers to all who thoughtfully view her work.[18] Complicated and contradictory, never perfect, the adventure of exploring the mind is not for the easily detoured or the faint of heart.

1 Ned Rifkin, "Agnes Martin–The Music of the Spheres," in *Agnes Martin: The Nineties and Beyond* (Houston: The Menil Collection, 2002), 25.
2 Rosalind Krauss, "The/Cloud/," in *Agnes Martin* (New York: Harry Abrams, Inc., 1992), 158.
3 Barbara Haskell, "Agnes Martin: The Awareness of Perfection," in *Agnes Martin* (New York: Harry Abrams, Inc, 1992), 93–117. Also consult Aline Brandauer, "Bearing Witness," in *Agnes Martin: Works on Paper* (Santa Fe: Museum of Fine Arts, 1998), 9–15.
4 Robert Goff, "Agnes Martin in Taos, New Mexico," *Western Interiors and Design* (July/August 2003): 87.
5 Donald Kuspit and Mark Van Proyen, "An Interview with Donald Kuspit—A Biographical Remark," in *Redeeming Art: Critical Reveries* (New York: Allworth Press, 2000), 310.
6 Agnes Martin, "The Untroubled Mind," *Writings* (New York: Distributed Art Publishers, Inc., 1991), 37.
7 Joan Simon, "Perfection Is in the Mind: An Interview with Agnes Martin," *Art in America* (May 1996): 88.
8 The fact that Martin claims the paintings speak for themselves in a language not made up of words should not cause anyone to avoid interpreting them. After all, artists throughout time and as varied as Michelangelo and John Marin have made exactly the same claim, allegedly to protect the integrity of the work. Thousands of articles and books later, Michelangelo's and Marin's art has not been diminished by the interpretative process.
9 Simon, 83.
10 Tom Collins, "Agnes Martin Reflects on Art and Life," *Geronimo* (January 1999): 11.
11 Martin, 15.
12 Martin, 29.
13 Holland Cotter, "Agnes Martin: All the Way to Heaven," *Art in America* (April 1993): 149.
14 Mary Lance, *Agnes Martin: With My Back to the World* (New Deal Films, Inc., 2002).
15 Martin, 68.
16 Martin, 70.
17 Martin, 141.
18 Martin, 71.

AGNES MARTIN

The Islands I–XII

gesso, synthetic polymer and graphite on canvas

6′ x 6′, 1979

Courtesy of the Whitney Museum
of American Art, New York.
Purchased with funds from
The Sondra and Charles Gilman, Jr. Foundation, Inc.
and Evelyn and Leonard A. Lauder

I

II

III

IV

V

VI

VII

VIII

IX

X

XI

XII

BECAUSE IT'S NOT
ONLY FOR ME;
IT'S FOR ALL THE PEOPLE.

—MARIA MARTINEZ

Marsha C. Bol

MARIA MARTINEZ
FOR ALL THE PEOPLE

WHEN I WAS FIVE YEARS OLD, MY FAMILY, LIKE SO MANY OTHERS, MOVED TO NEW MEXICO. THE FIRST NAME OF AN AMERICAN INDIAN THAT I LEARNED AS A YOUNG GIRL IN THE SOUTHWEST WAS NOT SITTING BULL OR GERONIMO. IT WAS MARIA.

No last name, just Maria, the potter. I learned about Maria from observing my mother. My mother, who had no ambitions as a collector of American Indian art or indeed of any type of art, admired the work of Maria. She wanted to own a piece of Maria's pottery. Mom's recognition of Maria's work made an impression on me, as my mother was not given to extolling objects in the world of art.

What was it that my mother so admired? In asking her this question recently, she replied that she thought Maria was "a perfectionist, who appeared to take a great deal of pride in her work. She made that special black pottery. It seemed that a lot of the potters catered to the tourists who wanted to buy inexpensive souvenirs to take home, but Maria never succumbed to that. She kept the quality. It must have taken a great deal of work to make her pots so smooth." My mother had heard the legendary story about Maria's "discovery" of the process of producing black pottery.[1]

Mom was not alone in her admiration. Maria Martinez's pottery has resonated with non-Indian people for one hundred years. In 1924 one admirer noted, "Among displays of Indian pottery I was particularly impressed with the work of an Indian woman, Maria Martinez."[2] Author Stephen Trimble remarked sixty years later, "At San Ildefonso, Maria Martinez and her sister Clara established an ideal in the early twentieth century. They could polish better than anyone, and as Maria's pots became a paragon, the family's high polish became a standard to meet."[3]

By 1924–25, when Ruth Bunzel conducted her landmark fieldwork among Pueblo potters, she called Martinez "the famous Maria."[4] How did this all begin, that a single individual woman potter, among all the many Pueblo potters, should become renowned for the perfection of her pottery?

Maria Montoya Martinez (c. 1887–1980) began making pottery as a young girl growing up in the Tewa-speaking Rio Grande Pueblo of San Ildefonso. Like all young Pueblo girls, she learned skills from a relative, observing her aunt, Nicolasa Montoya, as she worked the clay. Then Martinez experimented with the clay by herself, receiving instructive feedback on her initial efforts from her aunt. She made her pots for use at home: for cooking, food storage and to wash hair and mix bread dough.[5]

The same day that Maria married Julian Martinez, they left on a train to travel to the 1904 St. Louis World's Fair, where they were contracted to do performances in the Midway. There Martinez had her first experience demonstrating and selling her pottery to non-Indian people, spending her days making small bowls and jars to sell to the crowds of fair visitors. She noted the buyers' preferences, remarking that they selected her plain polished red bowls over other types that she had for sale.[6]

Beginning in 1907 archaeologists from the School of American Archaeology (later renamed the School of American Research), under the directorship of Edgar Lee Hewett, excavated a site on the Pajarito Plateau. They employed workers from San Ildefonso to assist. One of those workers was Julian Martinez. During the second field season, the couple was encouraged by Hewett, who was the director of both the school and the Museum of New Mexico, to reproduce the old pottery type from potsherds found at the site. Maria Martinez's obvious skill as a potter came to Edgar Hewett's attention. Thus began a long relationship between the Museum of New Mexico as patron and Maria and Julian Martinez as artists. As Maria recalled, "He [Edgar Hewett] was the one that we know first, and he was the one that start us in pottery [*sic*]."[7]

From 1909 to 1912 the wife-and-husband team became a living exhibition at the Museum of New Mexico, where they lived in the Palace of the Governors. Maria Martinez formed and polished pots daily, while her husband painted the designs, firing them in the courtyard of the Palace.

Even though Maria and Julian Martinez produced their pottery together, Maria is the recognized potter based on the Pueblo traditional gender division of labor. Pueblo people said that the women were the potters. Even though men could be seen painting and helping, sometimes even making an entire pot, it would still only be considered "helping out."[8]

Visitors to the museum purchased pottery directly from the artists, while the museum collected selected works as well. The museum officials made their preferences known to Martinez, as an excerpt from a letter written by curator Olive Wilson indicates: "[The museum staff] consider [Maria] the best of the pottery makers hereabout, and she knows that we expect her work always to reach a certain standard, so she brings us only good pieces."[9]

The conscious exertion of influence by Museum of New Mexico officials on Pueblo pottery-making standards developed into a formalized project. The events of this influence provide a well-documented roadmap of the impact of the patronage by non-Indians on the development of a Native American art form.[10] In 1920 two women left a project in the care of Edgar Hewett. Verra von Blumenthal and Rose Dougan had spent two summers trying to stimulate a high-grade pottery-making industry at San Ildefonso Pueblo, the products of which they intended to market throughout the United States. Von Blumenthal, who had promoted a similar revival in quality lacemaking throughout villages in Russia with some success, expected to implement the same plan at San Ildefonso. Finding that they were having little success at the Pueblo, the two women turned their project over to Hewett. He then appointed two museum staff, Kenneth Chapman and Wesley Bradfield, to undertake the project. Chapman and Bradfield developed the following criteria for effecting this quality improvement:

1. Inviting the potters to submit their wares to us at the Museum before offering them for sale elsewhere.
2. Asking each potter to set her price, piece by piece.
3. Selecting a few outstanding pieces, if any, and explaining why they were chosen (for form, finish, decoration, etc.).
4. Adding at least 25 percent to the price named by the potter for those selected, and promising still higher prices for further improvement.[11]

Chapman tells the story of the first application of their quality improvement formula:

> Julian and Maria Martinez of San Ildefonso appeared with a wagonload of pottery. Here was an unexpected problem. They were the last we would have picked for our experiment, for they were accomplished craft workers who might resent our suggestions for improvement of their wares. However, we knew they were forced to limit the time expended on each piece, for they had learned that the dealers would not pay higher prices for a more finished product. So, in hopes of finding one or more outstanding pieces in the lot, we decided to test our plan. It worked wonders!
>
> We set aside four unusually well-formed and finished pieces and asked their prices. Then we commended the couple for the attractive qualities of their pottery and paid 25 percent more than they had asked. That concluded, we told them of our plan and promised even more for others in their next lot if they showed further improvement.[12]

In Carl Guthe's 1925 study of pottery-making at San Ildefonso, Alfred Kidder, in writing the introduction, observed the actions of the museum:

> The authorities of the Museum of New Mexico and the School of American Research threw themselves heartily into the task of stimulating the industry . . . . The undertaking was not an easy one, however, for it was difficult to get most of the women to go to the trouble of making good pieces when the tourists, who were still the principal purchasers, were equally or even better pleased with imitations of china water-pitchers, ill-made raingods, and candlesticks. The problem thus resolved itself into one of supplying a market. The Museum bought many good pieces, and Mr. Chapman, who from the beginning had been a leading spirit in the attempt at rehabilitating the art, himself purchased large amounts of pottery, never refusing a creditable piece, never accepting a bad one . . . .
>
> Maria especially shone. By 1915 she had far surpassed all others, her pots were in great demand, and at the present time she has a ready market, at prices which ten years ago would have seemed fantastic, for everything she can find time to make.[13]

As Chapman reported, the Museum of New Mexico officials consciously initiated a consumer standard which they determined would be the desirable direction for the development of quality Pueblo pottery and the growth of a thriving market, encouraging Martinez to strive toward greater and greater technical perfection in her pottery-making. Martinez responded to the market-driven call for perfection by making pots that were increasingly technical marvels with seemingly mechanical precision of shape, sure-handed painting that belied the human touch and lustrous, unblemished polish. She remarked, "That's what people like, when I [make] the edge straight and perfect."[14]

Martinez took a risk investing her materials, time and energy in making a single piece, when the same investment could be used to make multiple simpler, less accomplished pieces whose sales were assured. However her risk paid off. The buyers showed up to purchase every piece that she produced—among them my mother, who responded to Martinez's decision to aim for perfection.

Chapman noted that the majority of the consumers of Martinez's pottery were women. "Most women who buy pottery are considering its use in their homes. Often I have heard a tourist say, particularly of Maria Martinez's polished, plain, or decorated black ware, 'How lovely! It doesn't look too Indian. It might have been made almost anywhere. I like it because it will fit in well with my other things, for use, and for its lovely form and finish.'"[15]

Today Martinez's pots can be found throughout the world—sitting on shelves in the home of artist Florence Pierce; in Fallingwater, the famed Frank Lloyd Wright–designed summer home of the Kaufmann family in western Pennsylvania; and in my mother's living room.

The lionization of Maria Martinez by the outside world was a first in the history of San Ildefonso Pueblo. Singling out of an individual genius artist for fame is a distinctly Western European concept in all ways in opposition to the Pueblo concept of the primacy of the group. Martinez as a traditional Pueblo woman faced the dilemma of coping with individual fame within her culture that valued the welfare of the entire community over the importance of the individual. Repeatedly, when dealers wanted to purchase only Martinez's pottery, she professed, "It all comes from San Ildefonso.... It's the pueblo that makes the difference, not the woman who makes the pottery."[16] When other potters of their village wanted to learn how to make the black pottery, the Martinezes shared the firing method with them so that everyone could benefit from its popularity.

In 1923 the superintendent of the Santa Fe Indian School proposed that Martinez sign her pots like Euro-American artists. Thus buyers could be assured they were purchasing her original work. Martinez, again confronted with the Western European homage of the individual named artist, negotiated this conflict with Pueblo group values by sharing her signature with other San Ildefonso potters. She signed their pots along with hers, so that all the pots would have an equal chance to sell. The signature exposes another basic difference between Western and Pueblo processes of artistic production. In Pueblo pottery-making, several members of the family usually collaborate in making a pot, from collecting and preparing the clay to molding, sanding, painting and firing. Thus most of Martinez's signed pots bear more than one name—hers plus another collaborating family member. Even so, it is Maria Martinez singly who remains the most famous Native American artist.[17]

Martinez's accomplishment of seemingly perfect pottery was a prime factor behind her artistic acclaim in the non-Pueblo world. It leads one to the question, Does perfection exist as a Pueblo concept or was it introduced to Martinez by her museum patrons? In a discussion of pottery-making, Tessie Naranjo, a Santa Clara Pueblo scholar, says that "the concepts of perfection and professionalism are of minimal importance in traditional Pueblo thinking." Naranjo speaks instead about the Pueblo concept of "do[ing] it the right way."[18]

If they "do it the right way," or correctly, the result is a collaboration, a relationship between the potter and the spiritual element of the clay. At its basis, this relationship between potter and "clay, which is of the earth, of the mother," hence a living thing, requires that the potter treat the clay with respect and reverence. In return for respectful treatment, the clay "will graciously allow herself to be taken by the people and will bless the potter by being moldable."[19]

Respectful treatment involves certain ritual actions. The relationship between potter and the living clay begins at the clay pit and continues throughout production of the pot. Before digging the clay at the pit, a potter says a prayer asking the clay to allow itself to be taken and offers corn meal. The potter converses with the clay while she coils and forms the pot. When she sands the pot to smooth it, the maker saves the sanded particles to use later in another pot. Should she carelessly toss the particles in the trash, the clay spirit would be offended and their relationship damaged.

The potter's attitude while she is working is extremely important. As one San Ildefonso potter says, "If you're angry and if you are making pots with bitter feelings toward others or towards something, your pots will act accordingly."[20] "If the pot is to be beautiful and proud, Clay-old-lady and the potter must collaborate," says Tessie Naranjo.[21]

Maria Martinez was a traditional Pueblo woman who formed full and deep relationships with her clay, making pots according to the Tewa philosophy of correctness. Her resulting beautiful pots gave evidence to her community that she was doing it "the right way." San Ildefonso potter Blue Corn recalled, "One time she told me to . . . pray every time when I go for some clay . . . . To know her, she was a really good lady."[22]

When Martinez learned pottery-making as a young girl from her aunt, Nicolasa Montoya instructed her to sprinkle corn meal and to say a prayer before she fired her pots. Much depended on the successful firing of the pots. If they broke during the firing, the entire effort was wasted. When Martinez's first jar came out perfectly from the firing, Montoya prophesied that her niece would always have good luck with firing because her very first piece turned out right.[23] According to the Tewa view of the world, the correctness of her process—her respect for the clay, her prayers and corn meal offerings to its spirit, her positive thoughts and deeds—influenced the outcome, the beautiful pot, whole and unblemished.

This same philosophy prevails in Pueblo ceremony. As Martinez's son, Popovi Da, explained it, "If the right persons are in the dance and preliminary ceremonies were done correctly, and the dance is carried on according to prescribed ritual, the rain will come."[24] Just as rain is the desired outcome of ritual, a fine pot is the desired outcome of the collaboration between the potter and her clay.

Maria Martinez shared her pottery-making knowledge with her community just as she had been taught by her aunt. Aunt Nicolasa "said that pottery-making belongs to everybody. Everybody who came to her and wanted to learn to make pottery, she taught. She said that was the way it was supposed to be. I want to do things right, the way she told me."[25] "Because it's not only for me; it's for all the people."[26]

1. For the story of Maria and Julian Martinez's rediscovery of black pottery and invention of the black-on-black pottery style, see Richard L. Spivey, *The Legacy of Maria Poveka Martinez* (Santa Fe: Museum of New Mexico Press, 2003), 7, 13, 17, 33–36.
2. Pedro J. Lemos, "The Household Arts of the Indian Pueblos," *El Palacio* 16:8 (1924): 128.
3. Stephen Trimble, *Talking With the Clay: The Art of Pueblo Pottery* (Santa Fe: School of American Research Press, 1987), 20.
4. Ruth L. Bunzel, *The Pueblo Potter: A Study of Creative Imagination in Primitive Art* (New York: Columbia University Press, 1929), 57.
5. Spivey, 172.
6. Alice Marriott, *Maria: The Potter of San Ildefonso* (Norman: University of Oklahoma Press, 1948), 120.
7. Spivey, 178.
8. J. J. Brody, personal communication, 1991; see also Marriott, 168.
9. As quoted in Jonathan Batkin, *Pottery of the Pueblos of New Mexico, 1700–1940* (Colorado Springs: Colorado Springs Fine Arts Center, 1987), 31–32.
10. Other examples of documented outside patronage in the Southwest include traders with Navajo weavers, and the archaeologist Jesse Walter Fewkes with Hopi-Tewa potter Nampeyo.
11. Kenneth M. Chapman, *The Pottery of San Ildefonso* (Santa Fe: School of American Research/University of New Mexico Press, 1970), 28.
12. Chapman, 29–30.
13. Alfred Kidder in Carl E. Guthe, *Pueblo Pottery Making: A Study at the Village of San Ildefonso* (New Haven: Yale University Press, 1925), 14.
14. Spivey, 175. Paradoxically, Martinez recognized that although her customers greatly admired her mechanical-like precision, they would not tolerate it if her pots were indeed mechanically produced. When asked if she would use the potter's wheel, Martinez replied, "Oh, if I try the wheel maybe the museum people will not like it." (Spivey, 181).
15. Chapman, 31. For further information on the gender of non-Native collectors of Native American art, see Marsha C Bol, "Defining Lakota Tourist Art, 1880–1915," in Ruth B. Phillips and Christopher B. Steiner, eds., *Unpacking Culture: Art and Commodity in Colonial and Postcolonial Worlds* (Berkeley: University of California Press, 1999), 222–25.
16. Marriott, 200.
17. Marriott, 233–35. For more information on Martinez's signatures, see Spivey, 161–66. For the construction of Martinez's fame, see Barbara Babcock, "Marketing Maria: The Tribal Artist in the Age of Mechanical Reproduction," in Brenda Jo Bright and Liza Bakewell, eds., *Looking High and Low: Art and Cultural Identity* (Tucson: University of Arizona Press, 1995), 124–50.
18. Tessie Naranjo, "Cultural Changes: The Effect of Foreign Systems at Santa Clara Pueblo," in Marta Weigle and Barbara A. Babcock, eds., *The Great Southwest of the Fred Harvey Company and the Santa Fe Railway* (Phoenix: The Heard Museum, 1996), 188–89.
19. Naranjo, 187–88.
20. Trimble, 14.
21. Naranjo, 189.
22. Spivey, 185.
23. Marriott, 26–27.
24. Spivey, 188.
25. Marriott, 223.
26. Spivey, 182.

MARIA MARTINEZ, Untitled, clay, 14.25″ x 11.5″, 1934
Courtesy of the School of American Research

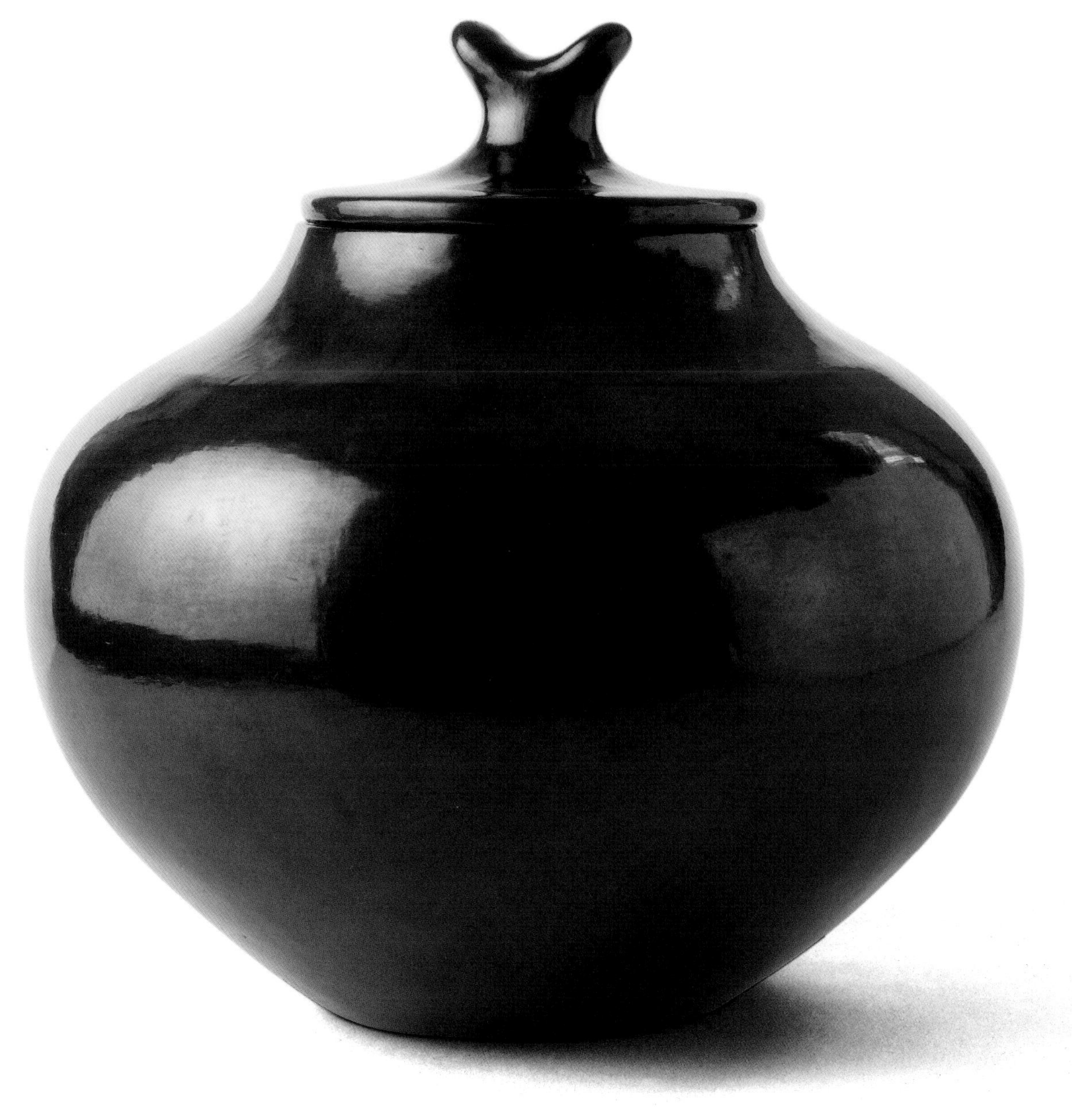

MARIA MARTINEZ AND JULIAN MARTINEZ, Untitled, clay, 12″ diameter, n.d.
Bequest of Rick Dillingham, Courtesy of the Museum of Indian Arts & Culture/Laboratory of Anthropology

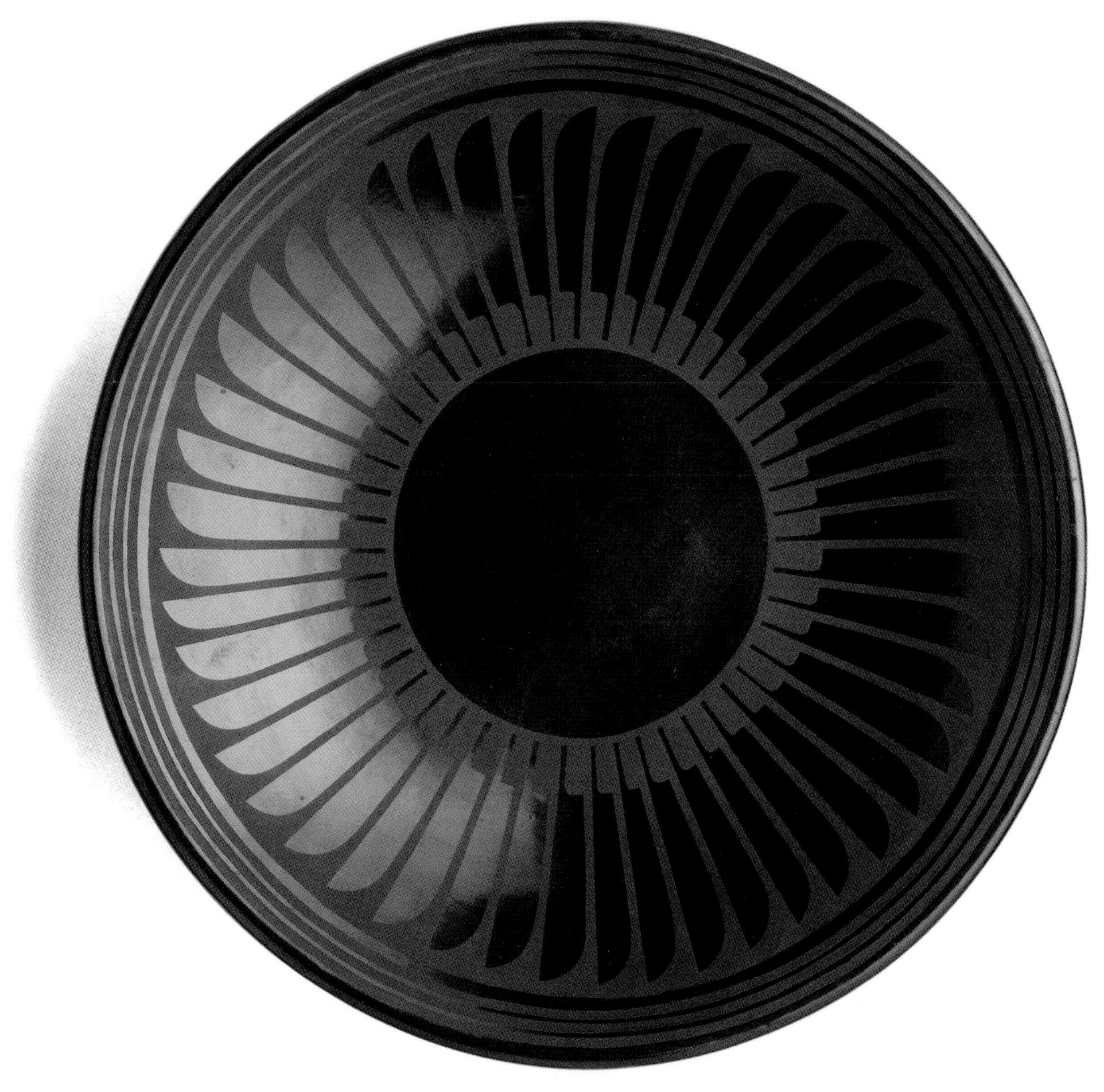

MARIA MARTINEZ AND POPOVI DA, Untitled, clay, 5" x 5.25", n.d.
Gift of Barbara Long, Courtesy of the Museum of Indian Arts and Culture/Laboratory of Anthropology

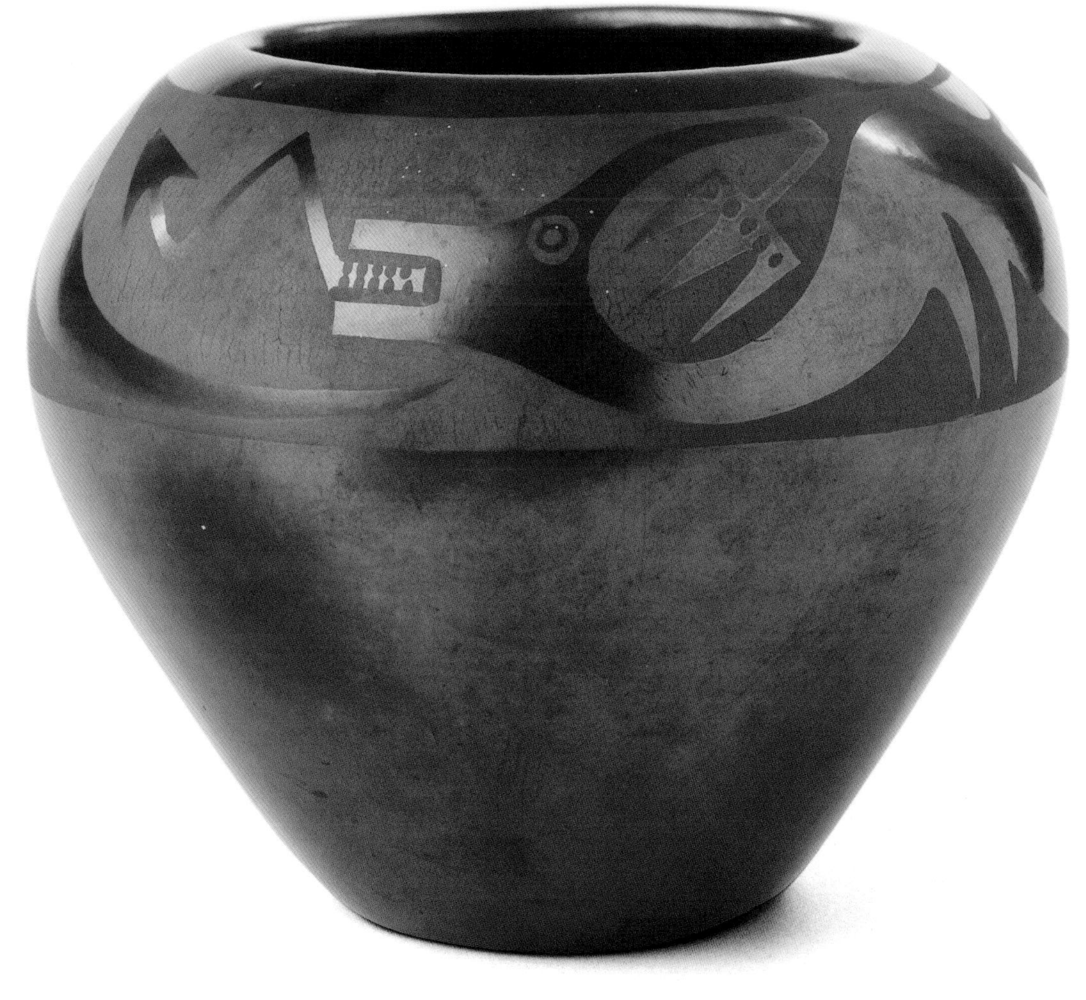

MARIA MARTINEZ AND JULIAN MARTINEZ, Untitled, clay, 10″ × 10″, n.d.
Museum Purchase, Courtesy of the Museum of Indian Arts & Culture/Laboratory of Anthropology

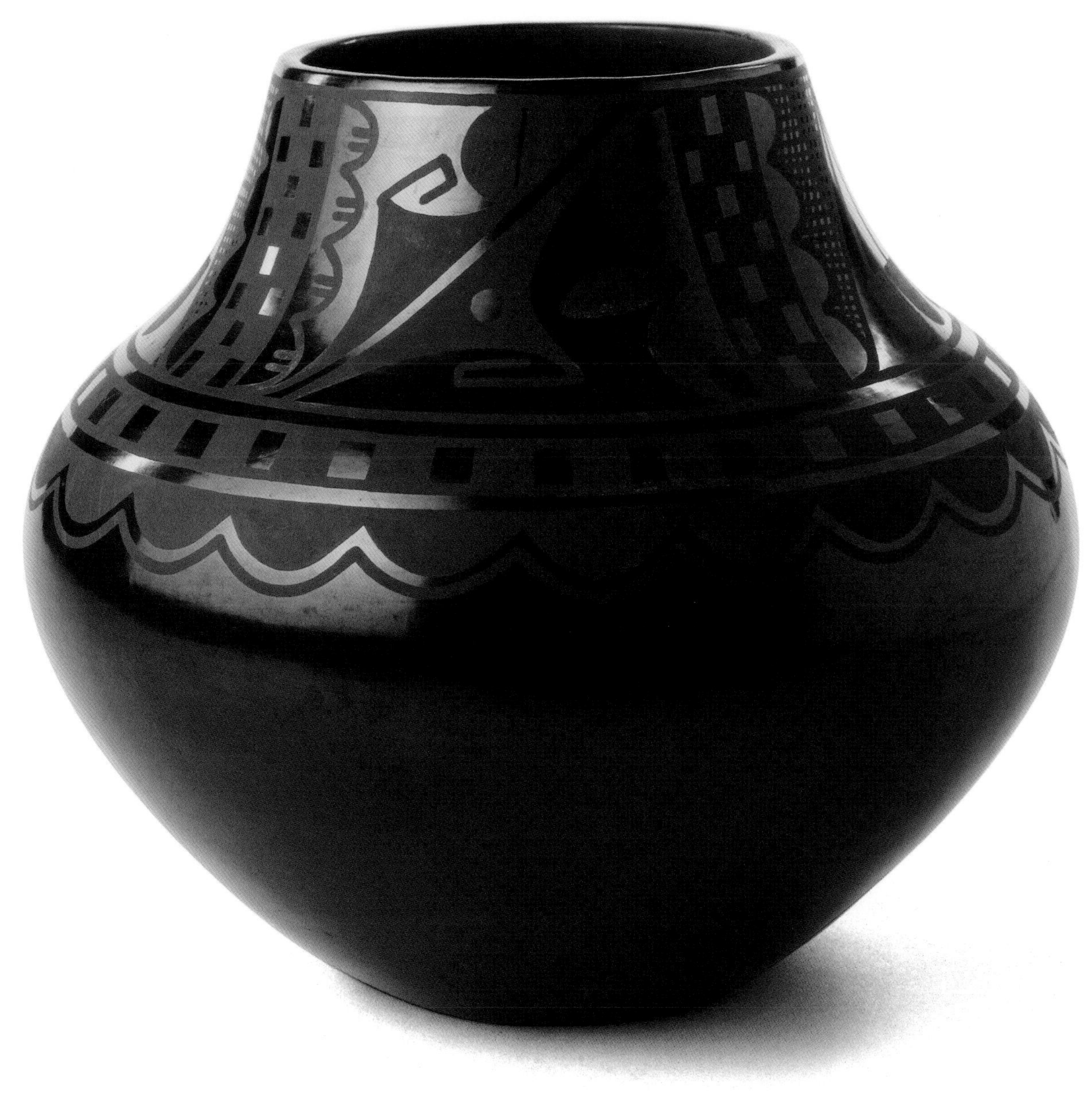

MARIA MARTINEZ AND POPOVI DA, Untitled, clay, 12″ diameter, n.d.
Gift of Barbara Long, Courtesy of the Museum of Indian Arts & Culture/Laboratory of Anthropology

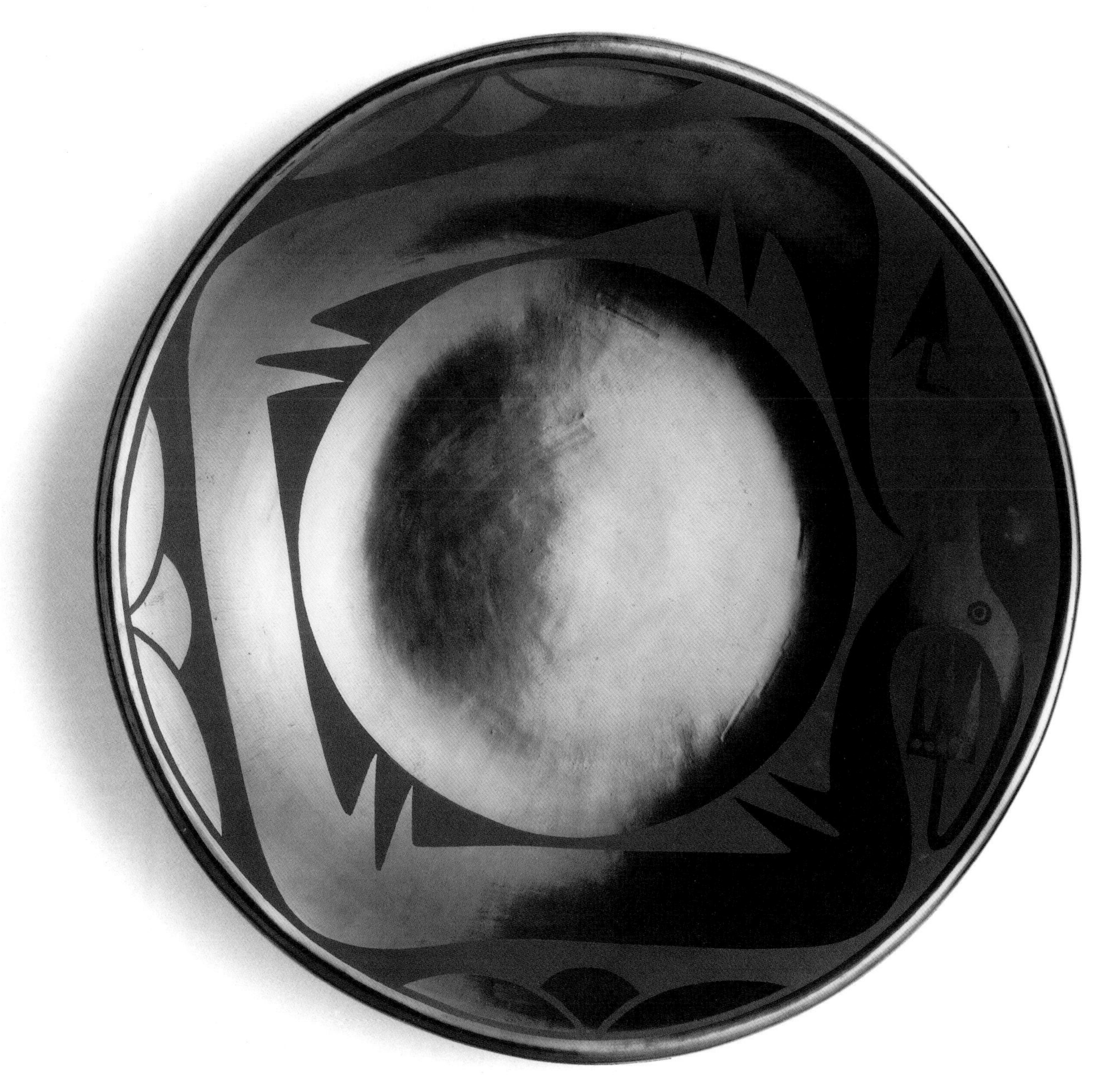

MARIA MARTINEZ AND JULIAN MARTINEZ, Untitled, clay, 10.5" x 9", n.d.
Museum Purchase, Courtesy of the Museum of Indian Arts & Culture/Laboratory of Anthropology

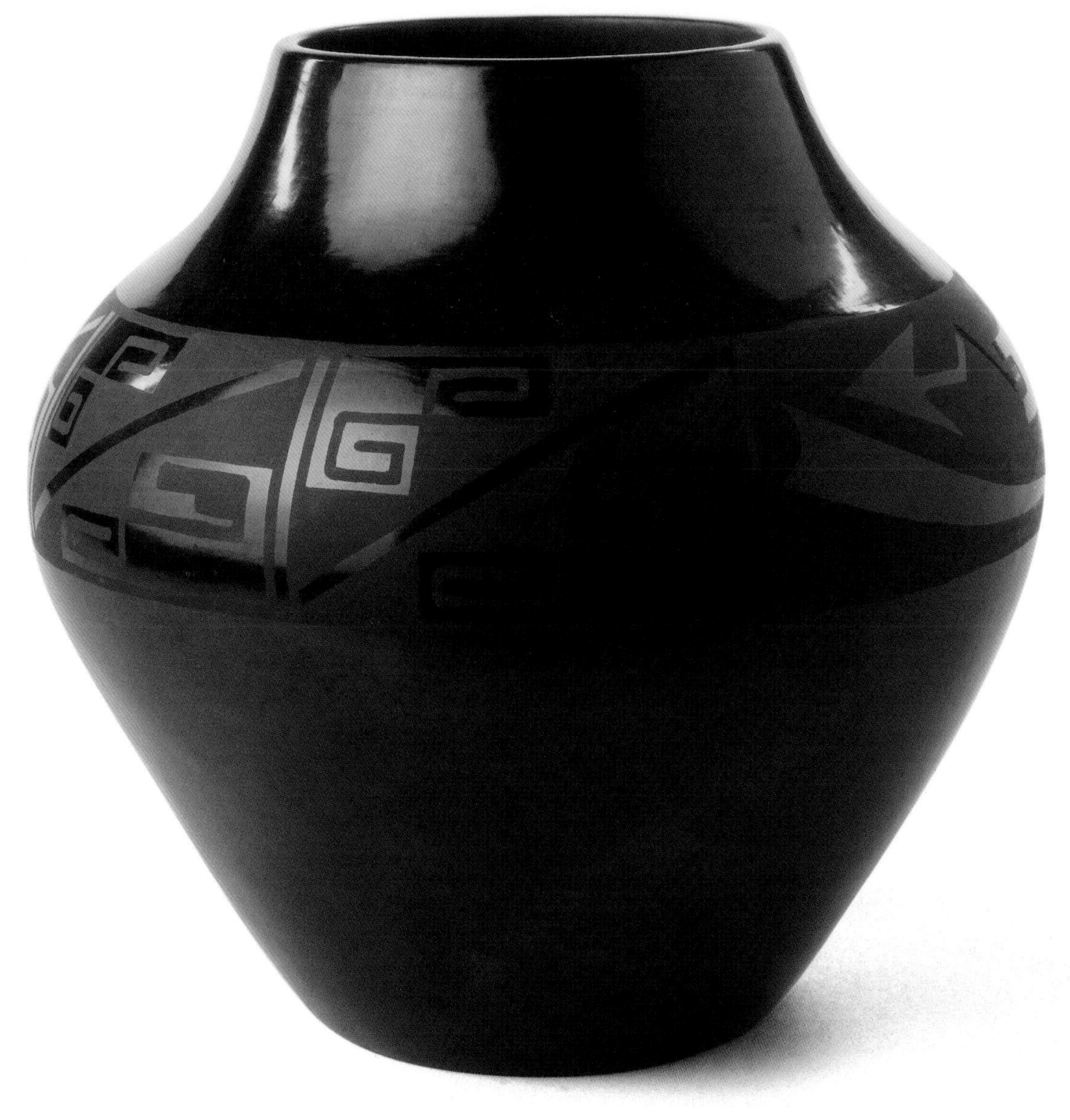

MARIA MARTINEZ AND SANTANA MARTINEZ, Untitled, clay, 4" x 4.5", c. 1956
Courtesy of Martha R. Clift

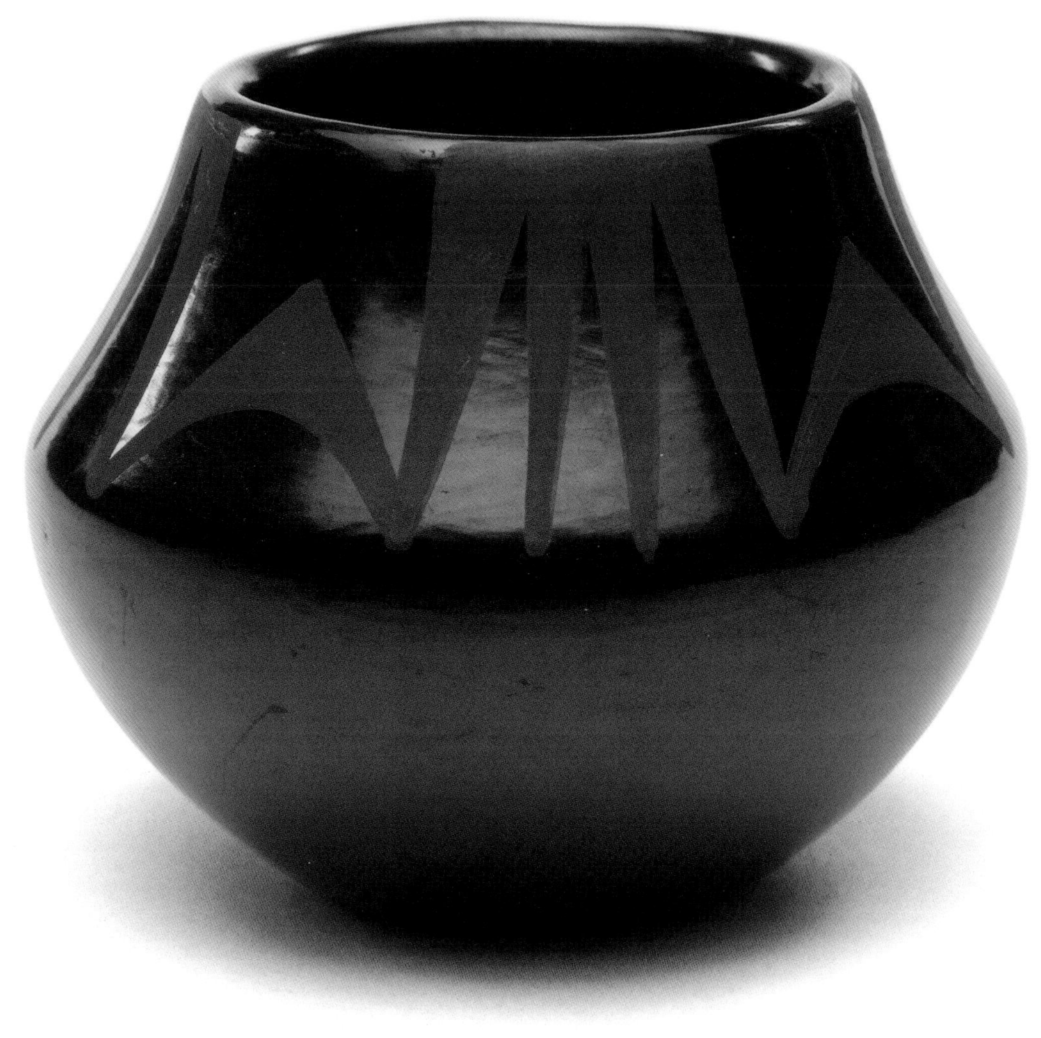

MARIA MARTINEZ AND SANTANA MARTINEZ, Untitled, clay, 5.25″ diameter, n.d.
Herman C. and Bina Ilfeld Collection in the Museum of Indian Arts & Culture/Laboratory of Anthropology

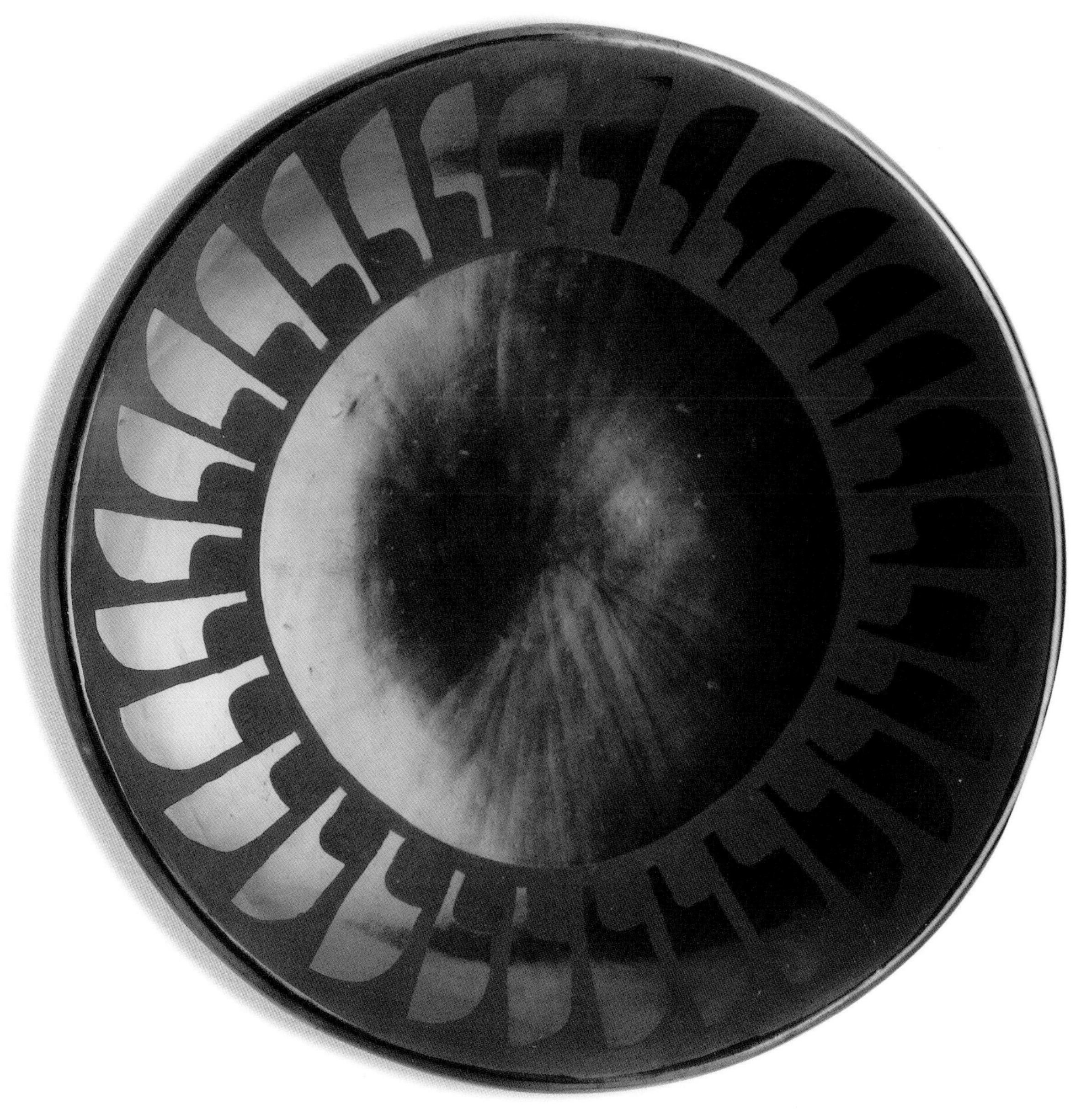

MARIA MARTINEZ AND JULIAN MARTINEZ, Untitled, clay, 5.5″ x 6.5″, n.d.
Herman C. and Bina L. Ilfeld Collection in the Museum of Indian Arts & Culture/Laboratory of Anthropology.

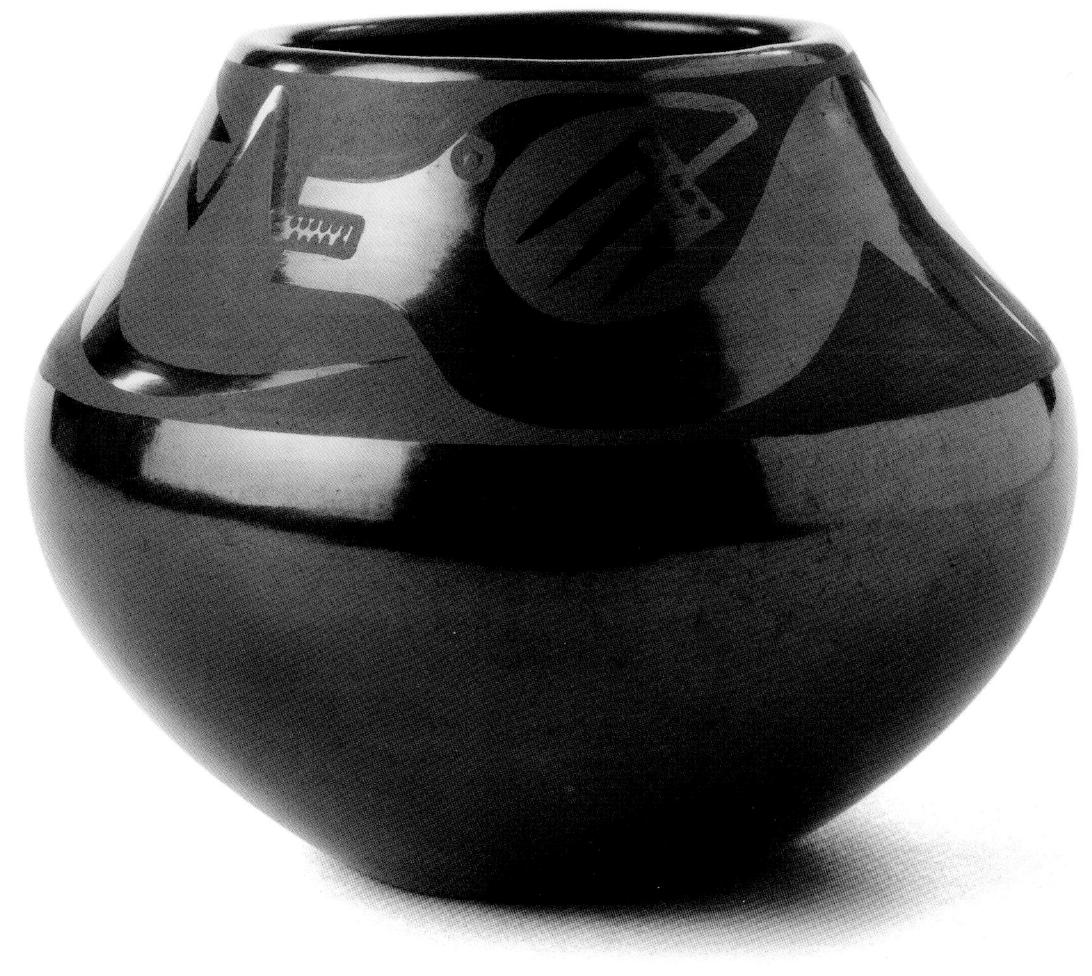

MARIA MARTINEZ, Untitled, clay, 6.125″ × 12″, 1967
Courtesy of the School of American Research

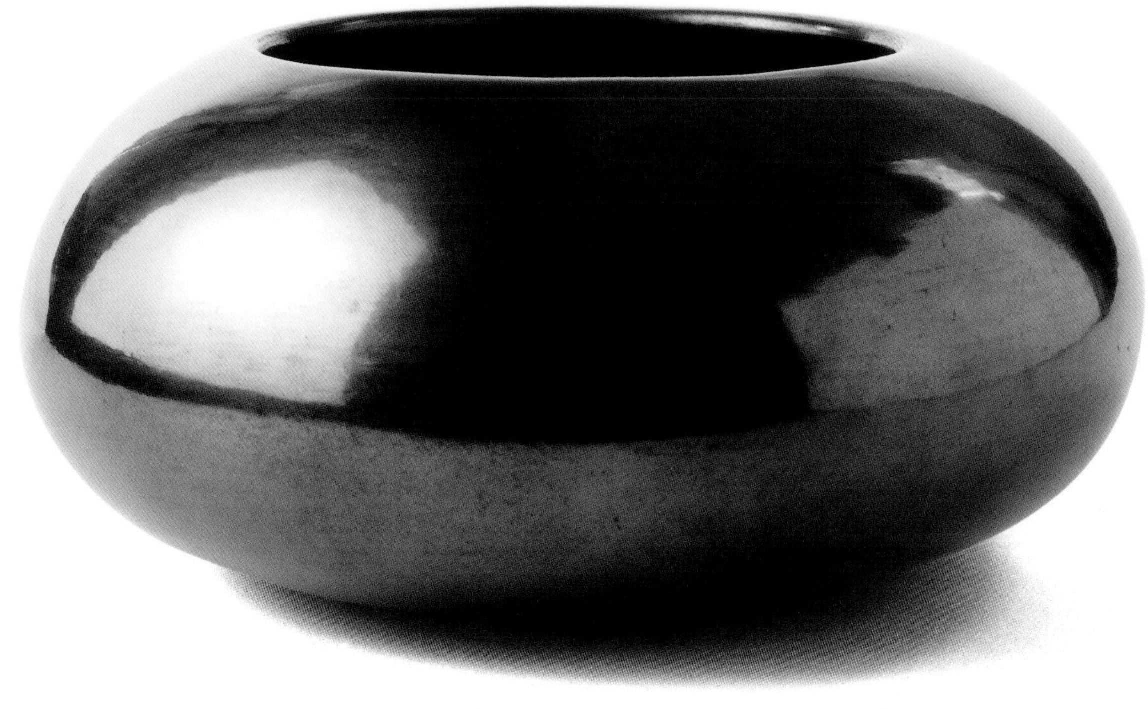

MY WORKS ARE CONTEMPLATIVE. THEY'RE ABOUT STILLING THE MIND.

—FLORENCE PIERCE

Lucy R. Lippard

TRAVELING LIGHT
FLORENCE PIERCE[1]

IN MOST CULTURES, LIGHT IS GENERICALLY ASSOCIATED WITH REVELATION, OR WITH DIVINITY—A KIND OF PERFECTION UNAVAILABLE AND SOMETIMES NOT EVEN BELIEVABLE TO THE MERE HUMAN. WHAT, AFTER ALL, CAN BE MORE BRILLIANT AND MORE WELCOME THAN LIGHT?

The light of day, the light at the end of the tunnel. They say death brings a white light; birth does too. While black is heavy, a burial, a density, an absorbing darkness, light is light, elusive, an epiphany, lifting us out of the grave. But Florence Pierce has created her own illuminations, and they are not so easily defined.

I can't think of Pierce's work without visualizing that unique glow—sometimes faint behind a stronger color, sometimes trapped as an undertone subtly giving way to a new chromatics, sometimes all-pervasive, sometimes blotchy, sometimes smoky, foggy, icy . . . . Her monochrome resin squares create their own weather. For some viewers, that weather in turn creates its own emotions, like the comings and goings of sun and clouds within the day.

Monochrome of any kind is a challenge for any painter. I've called monochromes "the silent art," and have long admired both Robert Ryman—the painter of white par excellence—and Ad Reinhardt—the painter of black par excellence. White is an absence, while black, although colorless, is the submerged presence of all colors. In Ryman's work the paint and the way it is laid on the surface manipulate the given light and provide the structure. In Reinhardt's work the inner cross structure and underlying colors are hidden in the shadows of an apparently overall matte black. Pierce's monochromes resemble neither, although she has something in common with Ryman's endlessly inventive way of using materials to play with inner and outer light, as well as something in common with Reinhardt's formal secrecy. The work of all three can be kindled and re-awakened or dimmed and deadened by installation decisions. Pierce's reliefs, especially the white ones, hung on white walls, seem to float in their own light-produced ether. Dennis Jarrett has written of Pierce's paintings, "depending on the strength and the angle of the light, they begin to breathe, to exhale color at you."[2] A sheet of vellum laid on top of the layers of resin over plastic mirror, and then removed, gives each work its final skin and takes the shine off the surface. Placed and then removed, it is a secret, like Reinhardt's shadowy crosses.

Pierce has made black resin ("licorice") reliefs as well as those in luscious colors, but her white works, selected for this show, were the first and remain the core of her monochrome years. White has played an important part in her life and art, representing a tabula rasa, new beginnings. In 1936, as a teenager from Washington, D.C., coming to New Mexico to study with Emil Bisttram, she returned to Taos in the middle of a snowstorm. "I could smell the white up there," she recalls.[3] Sixty years later Pierce told a reporter, "White keeps coming up in my work. I don't know what it relates to exactly. The great influences are things we can't describe too distinctly. But the best work I have been doing is white."[4] Elsewhere she said, "The whites are my favorite because I feel I've done the most with the least."[5]

Studying in Taos, Pierce recalls, "was quite a jolt for me, coming from a very conservative family—we were Presbyterian—to realize that there were other spiritual allusions that I had no idea about. We were caught up in the language we were exposed to, and the phrase 'the fourth dimension' was bandied about quite a bit—even though we had no idea what it meant. But the whole idea of working visually in abstraction is almost fourth dimensional."[6] For Transcendentalists, as Bisttram, Raymond Jonson and others then called themselves, light could express color, rhythm and form. The young artists read Kandinsky's *Concerning the Spiritual in Art* (a lifelong favorite of Georgia O'Keeffe's as well) and discussed Annie Besant's "thought-forms." Pierce was less intellectually inclined. She recalls her transcendentalist paintings as "very emotional and visionary" works that were then ruined by Bisttram's insistence on adding symbols.[7] (The symbols didn't take, but years later, the early resin pieces initially incorporated circles, triangles and squares—the forms encouraged in her youth by Bisttram and his fellow Transcendentalists.) Also in the late 1930s, Pierce saw Brancusi's *Bird in Space* at the Museum of Modern Art in New York City, which she says was a major influence.[8] Peggy Lee, reviewing a 1939 exhibition of the Transcendentalists, noted that Miller (Pierce's maiden name) "admits an emotional motivation through which she is attempting to delve beyond the bonds of matter."[9] What finally happened is that rather than "delv[ing] beyond the bonds of matter," it was matter itself that brought Pierce to the kind of revelation Besant and others recommended. "Art first and think later" is her motto: "I want to travel mentally light."[10]

The Zen principle of welcoming accident and exploiting disorientation is at the heart of Pierce's discovery of her own path. She describes the epiphany she experienced when a drop of resin fell onto a bit of aluminum foil, an accident that eventually changed her art and her life: "I could manipulate resin and when I held it up to the light I found it itself was full of light."[11] The Buddhist principles of contemplation, of conscious breathing, and acting in the moment inform her work process, though Pierce says she is not a Buddhist. She is drawn to Zen-inspired Chinese painting, and at times to Zen practice. "The key is emptiness," she says. "Working is facing the void, or infinity. I no longer concern myself with design. It's not about anything. It just is .... I start every day by just looking at a blank square. There are mental states that come from the stilling of the mind, the quieting of the mind. I remember the Zen koan, 'Before you were born, what was your original face?' I've been regarding these squares as my original face."[12]

It was not until 1994 that she mused, "I think that spirituality has entered my work, but I'm scared to death of the word spirituality. And I've decided recently not to use that word, because it carries a lot of baggage with it."[13] She has been hard put to keep this promise, as it is a word that comes up frequently around her work, especially in New Mexico, especially in Santa Fe. She has, however, maintained her independence, her own subliminal senses of meaning.

Perhaps Pierce's squeamishness about the word *spirituality* when used loosely (which I happen to share) has something to do with her respect for Native American belief systems. When she was a student in Taos, she was barely aware of the nearby Pueblo's unique presence, because her teacher dismissed it as merely "primitive." "Bisttram never encouraged us to look at Pueblo culture," she says. "He was very condescending about it, even though he painted pueblo pictures that were very interesting. He did not have any warm feelings as far as I can recall about all that stuff."[14] Later she went to the ceremonial dances every year. "That's the way that this country would influence a person like myself at that age was going into a plaza and seeing all this non-Christian stuff .... We were just infused by the whole atmosphere." After Horace Pierce's death, Florence took two courses with anthropologist Florence Ellis at the University of New Mexico and found friends at Jemez Pueblo who allowed her a glimpse of the ways in which the ceremonial cycles pervaded their lives. She also read Joseph Campbell and James Hillman, at a time when her affinity for snakes (she once had two bullsnakes, named Adam and Eve, as house pets) helped her perceive the power of Avanyu, the horned water serpent. "I was acquiring all these serpents. I had real serpents and I had dream serpents, and I had serpent carvings that were given to me by Indian people .... I always felt so sorry for that serpent in Genesis ...."

What Pierce liked most was "the spiritual secrecy of the Indians." She was attracted to the fact that "there are still art forms around that come from a collective, sort of a collective soul," but is well aware that her own work comes from another source. In 1986 she made a pair of shaped resin panels which she called *Prayer Sticks*, after the fact ("because they looked so much like them . . . . I have a lot of prayer sticks that are authentic and some replicas"), and in the next decade she occasionally broke the black framing band on a series of white reliefs, in homage to the "spirit openings" in Pueblo pots or Navajo weavings. In the mid-1990s she was looking at Navajo sand paintings, and was particularly drawn to a *Whirling Logs* from the Nightway ceremony. But she has never directly emulated or incorporated anything from Native cultures. Primarily, it is the Native life that has been breathed into the place itself that has played a major role in Pierce's art. "An education is not so much what you get but *where* you get it," says Pierce. "The longest love affair I've had in my life has been with New Mexico."[15]

Like so many New Mexicans, Pierce attended the seasonal Pueblo dances, gaining a kind of empathetic understanding of the bonds between religion and nature celebrated there and perhaps also sensing the extended sense of time that characterizes Pueblo belief: "And then you become aware of the square on the plaza, and the duality of the kiva life, those two sets of dances, the winter dances, the summer dances, over and over again."[16] The dances themselves and the drumming and chants that accompany them are mesmerizing, as repetition transcends itself to evoke a sense of time that is unfamiliar to Western culture. Far more than any brief and belated exposure to New York Minimalism, this experience is responsible for Pierce's immersion in a repetitive process and subtle variation that induce a similar loss of linear time within the viewing experience.

Artists with contemplative goals proceed very differently from those who are thinking in theoretical terms, although the final products may look similar to others. After bucking the mainstream tides in New Mexico for years, Pierce eventually found herself an unconscious leader in a tributary where monochrome and what I used to call "rejective art" remain alive and well (in large part thanks to the art dealer Charlotte Jackson, Pierce's agent and rejective art's greatest local champion). There are a number of respected "minimalists" working in Santa Fe, Taos and Albuquerque, many of them women of various ages who share Pierce's aesthetic; Susan Wing, Christine Patten, Susan York, Gloria Graham, Mala Breuer, Anne Cooper, Connie de Jong and Joan Watts come to mind . . . and of course Agnes Martin. I suspect each of them credits to some extent the famous clarity of New Mexico's light, though this landscape affects everyone differently . . . and the light is dulling with urban sprawl and climate change.

It was not until the 1980s, when Pierce was already in her sixties, that she found "the geometry of light" she had sought for so long. And it was not until the early 1990s that she truly began to make "transcendental" art, moving past her own education and history. "A few years ago," she said in 1996, "I did this series of white pieces with the illusion of a line. It was the closest I could get to that void that Buddhists talk about."[17] Each one of this series of square white resin reliefs had a subtle vertical "line" created by a single fold in the vellum paper below the layers of clear resin; each was in a different place and the series itself, hung together, created a line across space, in and out of the paintings. Like a true New Mexican, she also brought her abstraction back to nature, seeing this series "like rain metaphorically—a single line of rain and movement across the surface."[18] But she did not follow this very successful direction, because the folds also destroyed the unity of the single square. "The square is very important to me," she says. "It has a magnificent presence all by itself. So I want to do as little as possible in it."[19]

"I thought I was at the end of my string when I did that work," Pierce says. "I didn't know what else I could do that would be satisfying. So I started working with colors . . . . Color is very emotionally lush, no matter what color you use. It isn't mysterious or ineffable. With opaque white there is nothing going on."[20] "Just as I thought to myself 'you don't need color,' boom, in came color . . . . I am pushing the density of the color, going as far away from the light without killing it—like the night sky."[21] While white may be considered purity personified, Pierce once made an intriguing statement about the way she tries to use color the same way: "not color as coloring but as the purest hue that I can get."[22] She succeeds in ways denied artists using paint as their vehicle to purity; since paint itself has such a powerful materiality, it does not disappear, bowing to light, the way the layered resin can.

Pierce has literally felt her way into her mature work over many years, arriving late, but not too late, at the vortex of form and emotion she was looking for, which she discovered through sensuous experience far more than through any specifically formal ambitions. If white and the square represent purity, they co-exist with a far more sensuous element—the resin itself and the process. "Resin is clear as water, thick as honey."[23] "When I'm not pouring, I'm thinking about pouring."[24] One critic observed that Pierce's "visual seductiveness gives weary 'minimalism' a voluptuous twist."[25]

There is not much point in discussing Pierce's work *as* Minimalism.[26] Departing from a very different point, she arrived there long after the movement had morphed several times. The relationship of minimal means and process to the pursuit of "perfection" has been more or less critically imposed after the fact. In the sense that any artist in the studio wants to make a perfect work, it is certainly valid. But "less is more" (or as Pierce has put it, "Less is more, unless it's a bore."[27]) is really about getting down to the bare bones of artmaking and lived perceptual experience. Pierce's brand of sensuous purism, often found in women's work, is perhaps closer to a 1966 exhibition I curated called "Eccentric Abstraction," in which I was looking for an alternative to hardline Minimalism. Soon afterwards, feminist artists based in Minimalism began to tease, alter and destroy the grid at the heart of much Minimal art, rethinking the notion of repetition in terms of traditional arts and tasks, and bringing content and emotion back into play while maintaining some of the formal structures, such as the modular armature. In a sense Pierce's glow serves a similar function.

If perfection is understood as purism, Pierce probably never intended to qualify. In fact it is the imperfections—the air bubbles, the pooling resin, the paper ripples, the unpredictable flows, the almost ragged edges—that make her art unique. In 1996 she did title some paintings *Pure Red* and *Pure Blue*, but she probably meant it as an homage to the depth and power of the colors rather than as any kind of finality. She has said that monochrome is "the purest and most abstract way to use color because you're not coloring."[28] Perfection, as the title of this exhibition suggests, is by definition out of reach. It is the pursuit, the longing to create more and more powerful objects with less and less visual fanfare, that makes Pierce and Martin so compelling. (Maria Martinez's brilliance was deeply embedded in a culture that did not need to consider such terms.) One of the tests of art as subtle as theirs is whether or not the intensity of the making experience is transmitted to the viewer, to the looking experience. Although these two sides of the aesthetic coin cannot really be compared, Pierce passes the test. She conveys to her viewers the transcendent pleasure she takes in being an artist. Asked how she would define her work, she replied, "As my reality. It is concerned with turning inward and toward the mysterious and unformed. It is non-objective, with no connection to politics, religious or social interest of our times . . . . My intent is to make art that is pristine, pure and timeless, which for me is the frank pursuit of beauty and joy."[29]

1 In this essay I have departed from, and sometimes echoed, my book *Florence Pierce: In Touch with Light* (Santa Fe: The Smith Book Fund/Palace Press International, 1998).
2 Dennis Jarrett, "The Unthinkable Florence Pierce," *Pasatiempo (The New Mexican)* (Feb. 9, 2000): 56.
3 Betty Ann Brown and Arlene Raven, *Exposures: Women and Their Art* (Pasadena: New Sage Press, 1988), 110.
4 Lis Bensley, "The 48" (interview), *Pasatiempo* (April 25, 1997): 4.
5 Emiliana Sandoval, "Effervescent resin reliefs that seem to float," *Pasatiempo* (Oct. 14, 1994).
6 Gussie Fauntleroy, "Spontaneous Production," *Pasatiempo* (March 21, 1997): 32–33.
7 Pierce in conversation with the author, 1996.
8 MaLin Wilson's notes on a conversation with Pierce, 1986; Jonson Gallery archives, UNM.
9 Peggy Lee, *New Mexico Lobo* (April 22, 1939).
10 Pierce in conversation with the author, 1996.
11 Kristen Hinrichs, "Profiles: Florence Pierce," *Charlotte Jackson Fine Art News* (Spring 1994).
12 Jarrett, 56.
13 Pierce, quoted in *The Magazine* (Oct. 1994): 17.
14 All quotations from Pierce below, concerning Pueblo culture (and snakes), are from the transcript of an interview with Pierce by Joseph Traugott and Cynthia Leyba, Sept. 5, 1995, in Jonson Gallery archives, UNM, Albuquerque, 19–21.
15 "A Dialogue with New Mexico Women Artists," catalogue for *Daily Bread: Art from Female Experience* (Albuquerque: University of New Mexico Printing Plant, 1983).
16 Traugott/Leyba interview, 21.
17 Bensley, 4.
18 Hinrichs.
19 Bensley, 4.
20 Bensley, 4.
21 Kathleen McCloud, "Florence Pierce's seamless process of creating," *Pasatiempo* (Dec. 6, 1996): 17.
22 Hinrichs.
23 Bensley, 4.
24 *The Magazine* (Oct. 1994): 17.
25 Jarrett, 56.
26 I did so in the book on Pierce.
27 Traugott/Leyba, 68.
28 *The Magazine*, 17.
29 Bensley, 4.

FLORENCE PIERCE, *Untitled,* number 271, resin on mirrored plexiglass, 16" x 16", 1998
Courtesy of Florence Pierce and Charlotte Jackson Fine Art, Inc.

FLORENCE PIERCE, *Untitled,* number 67, resin on mirrored plexiglass, 16″ x 16″, 1992
Courtesy of Mr. Thomas P. Lang, Jr.

FLORENCE PIERCE, *Untitled,* number 89, resin on mirrored plexiglass, 16″ x 16″, 1993
Courtesy of Florence Pierce and Charlotte Jackson Fine Art, Inc.

FLORENCE PIERCE, *Untitled*, number 87, resin on mirrored plexiglass, 24″ x 24″, 1993
Courtesy of Florence Pierce and Charlotte Jackson Fine Art, Inc.

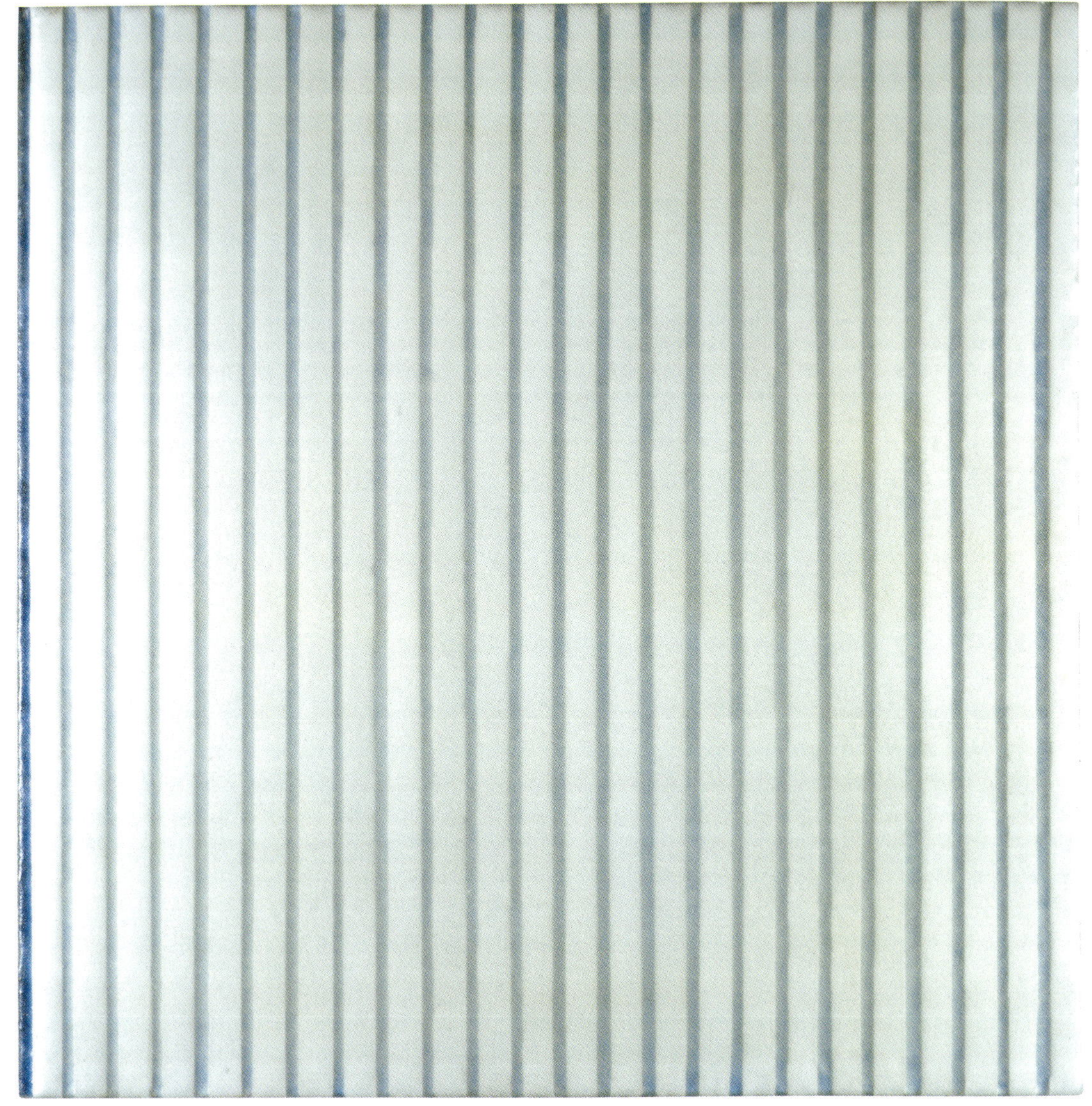

FLORENCE PIERCE, *Untitled,* number 190, resin on mirrored plexiglass, 24″ x 24″, 1996
Courtesy of Florence Pierce and Charlotte Jackson Fine Art, Inc.

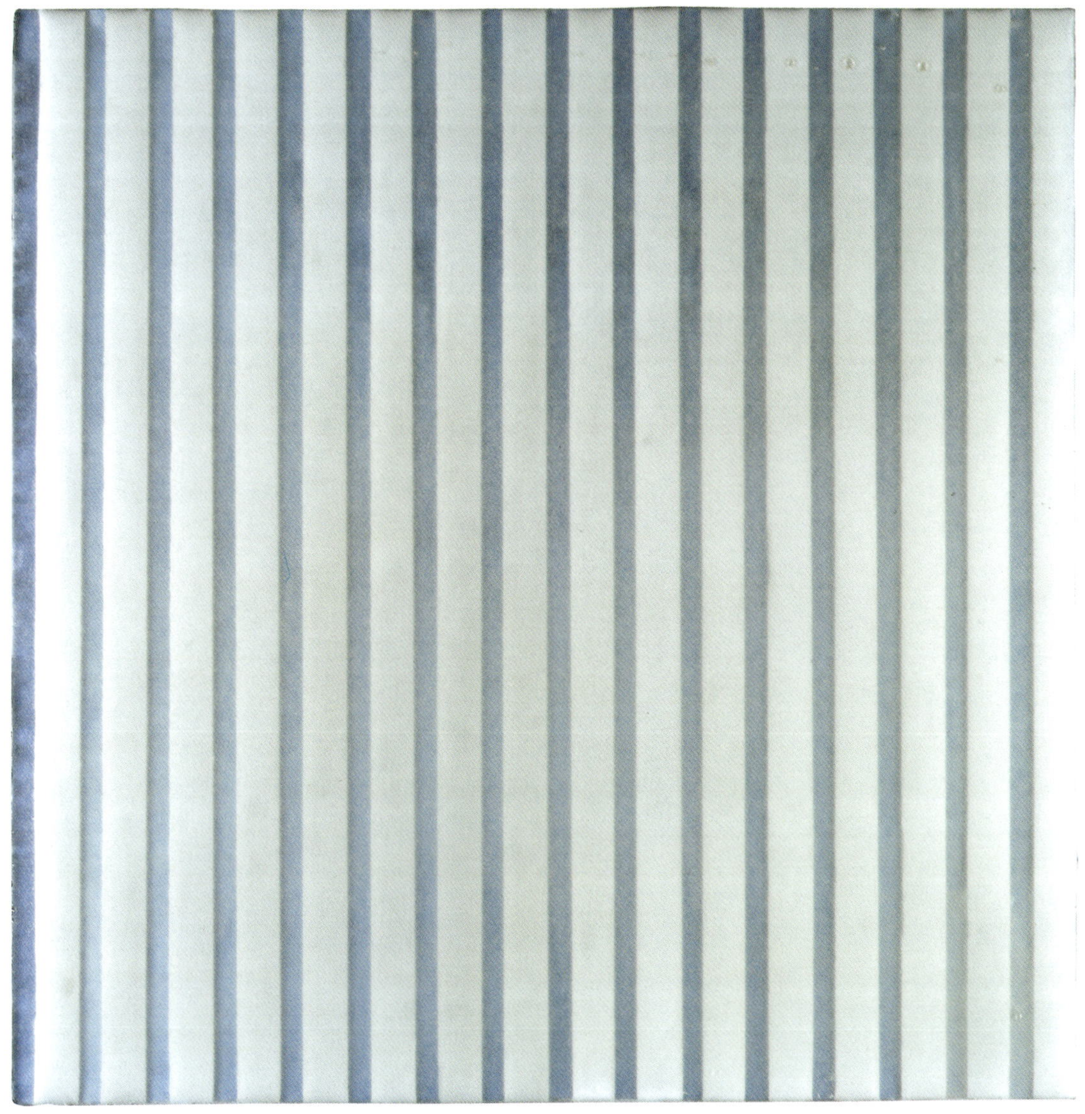

FLORENCE PIERCE, *Untitled,* number 81, resin on mirrored plexiglass, 16″ x 16″, 1992
Courtesy of Florence Pierce and Charlotte Jackson Fine Art, Inc.

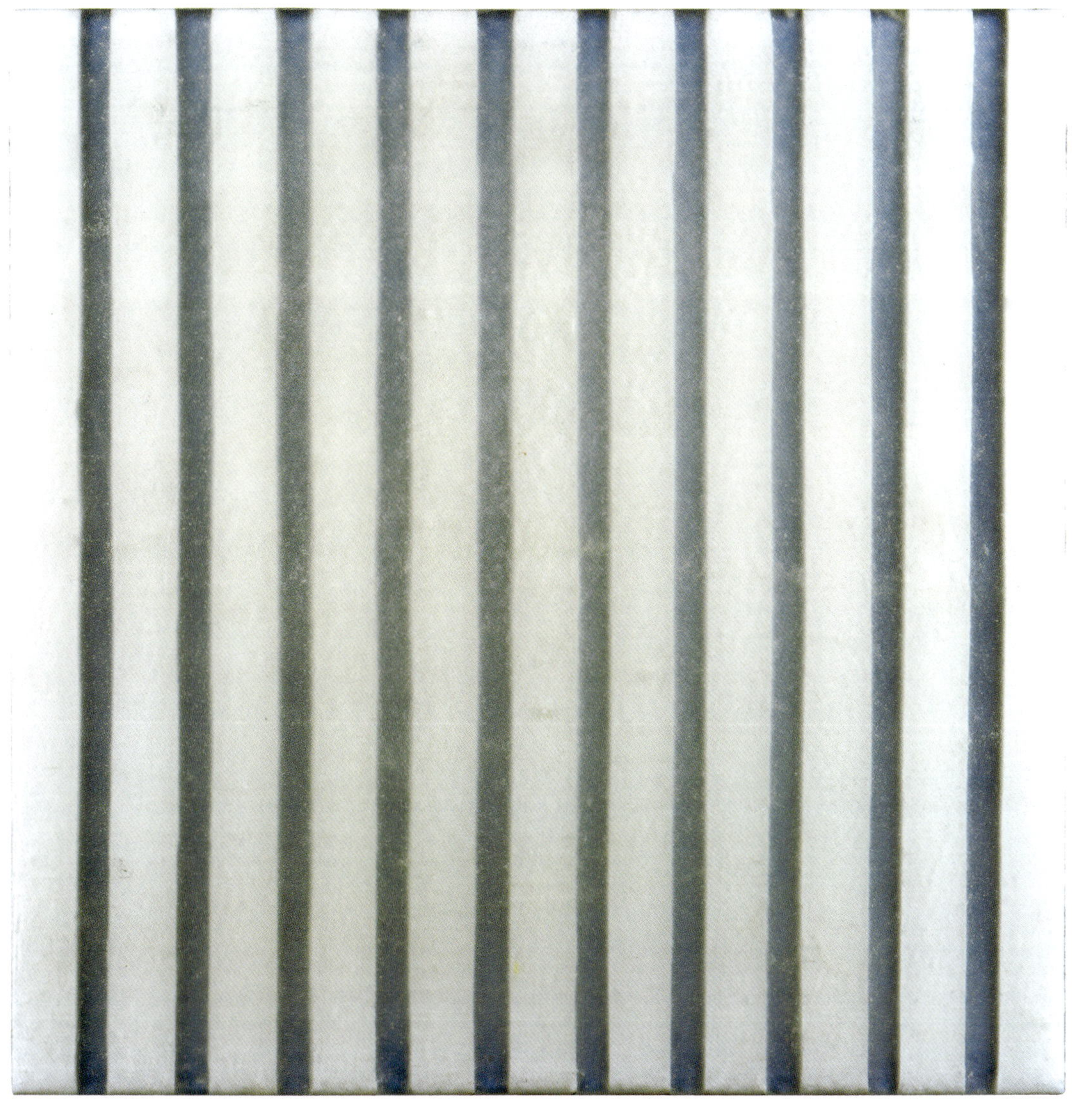

FLORENCE PIERCE, *Untitled*, number 8, resin on mirrored plexiglass, 16″ x 16″, 1990
Courtesy of Florence Pierce and Charlotte Jackson Fine Art, Inc.

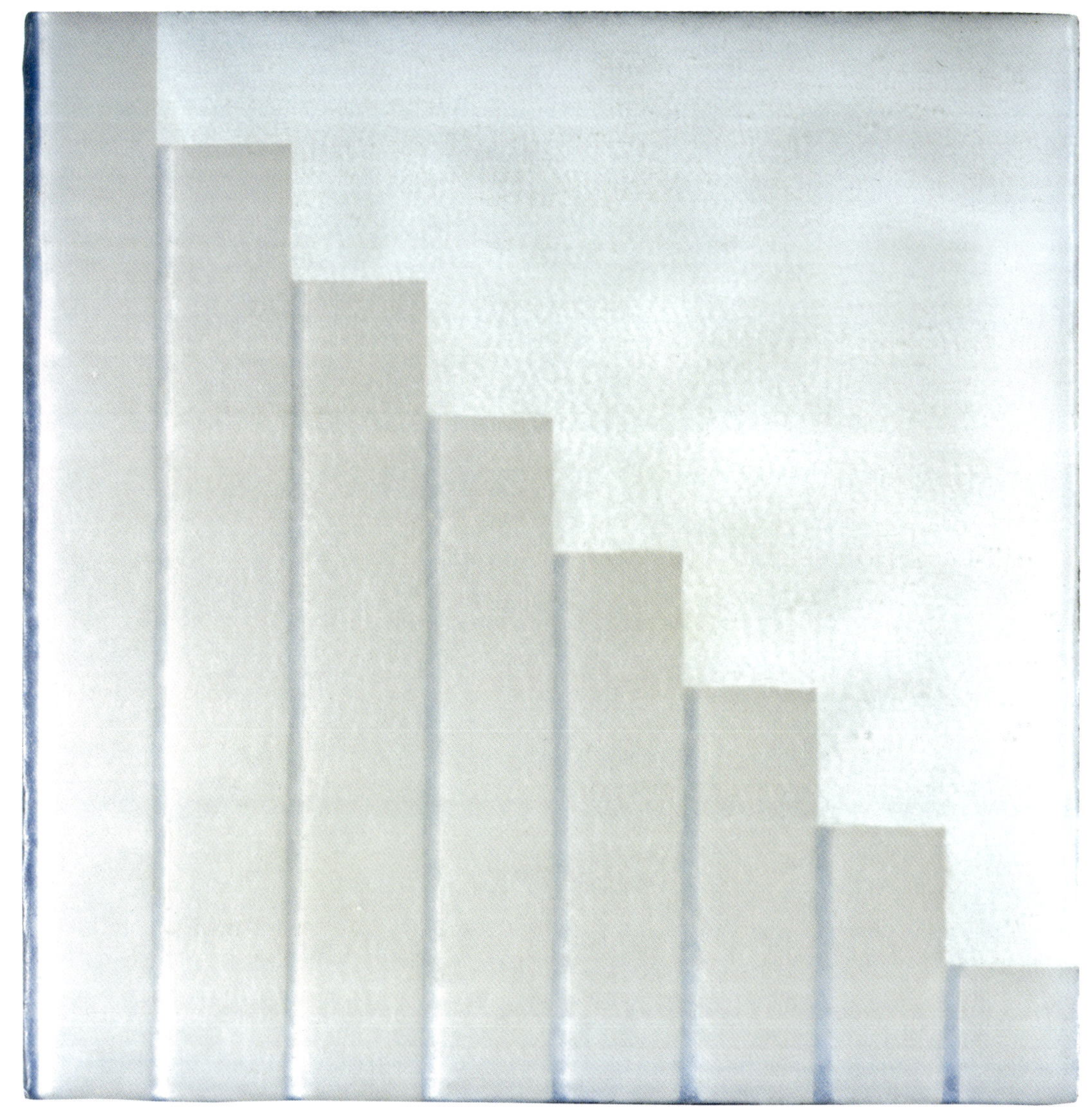

FLORENCE PIERCE, *Untitled,* number 280A, resin on mirrored plexiglass, 16″ x 16″, 1998
Courtesy of Florence Pierce and Charlotte Jackson Fine Art, Inc.

FLORENCE PIERCE, *Untitled,* number C35, resin on mirrored plexiglass, 24″ x 24″, 1994
Courtesy of Florence Pierce and Charlotte Jackson Fine Art, Inc.

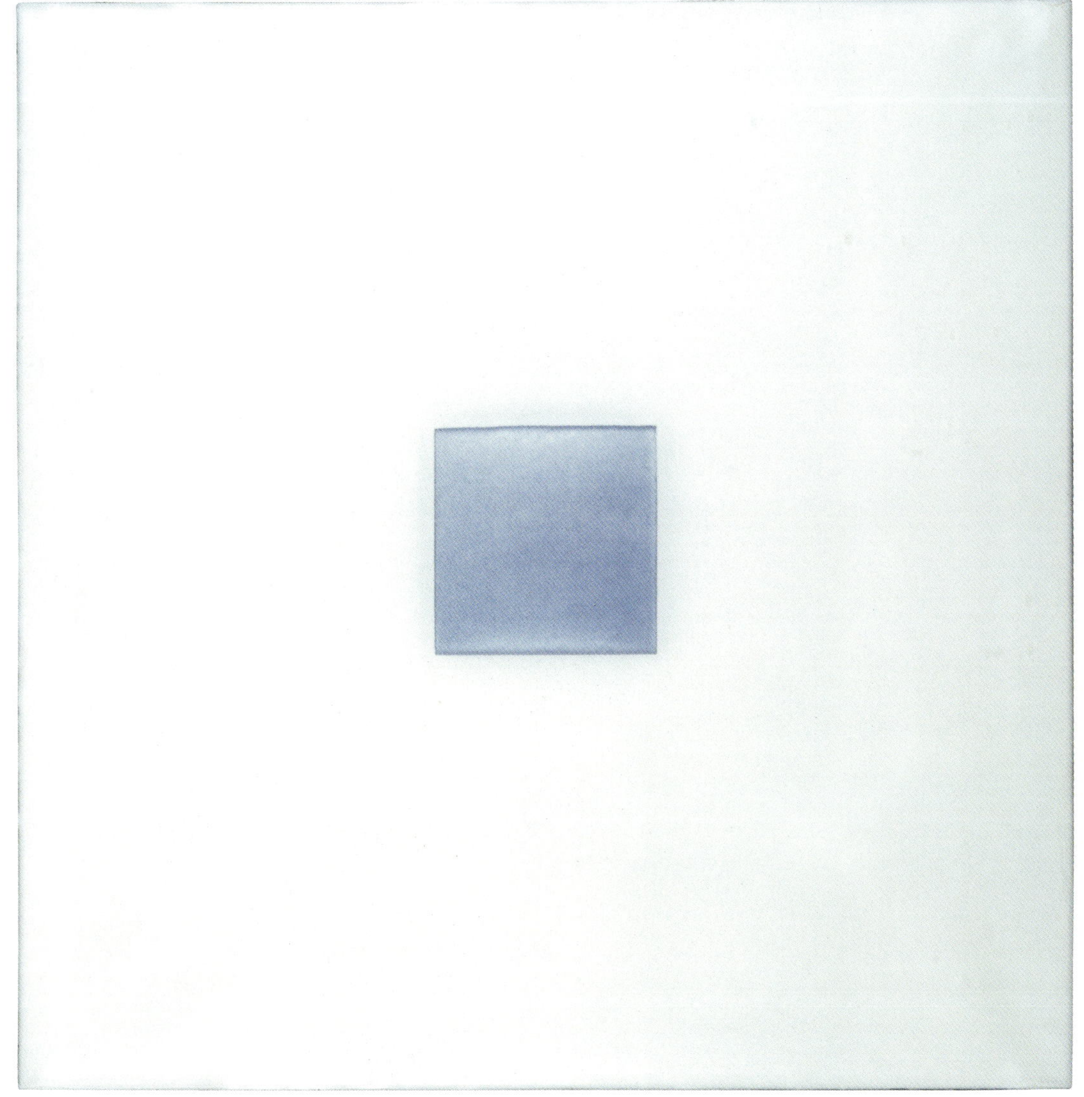

FLORENCE PIERCE, *Untitled,* number 73, resin on mirrored plexiglass, 24" x 24", 1995
Courtesy of Florence Pierce and Charlotte Jackson Fine Art, Inc.

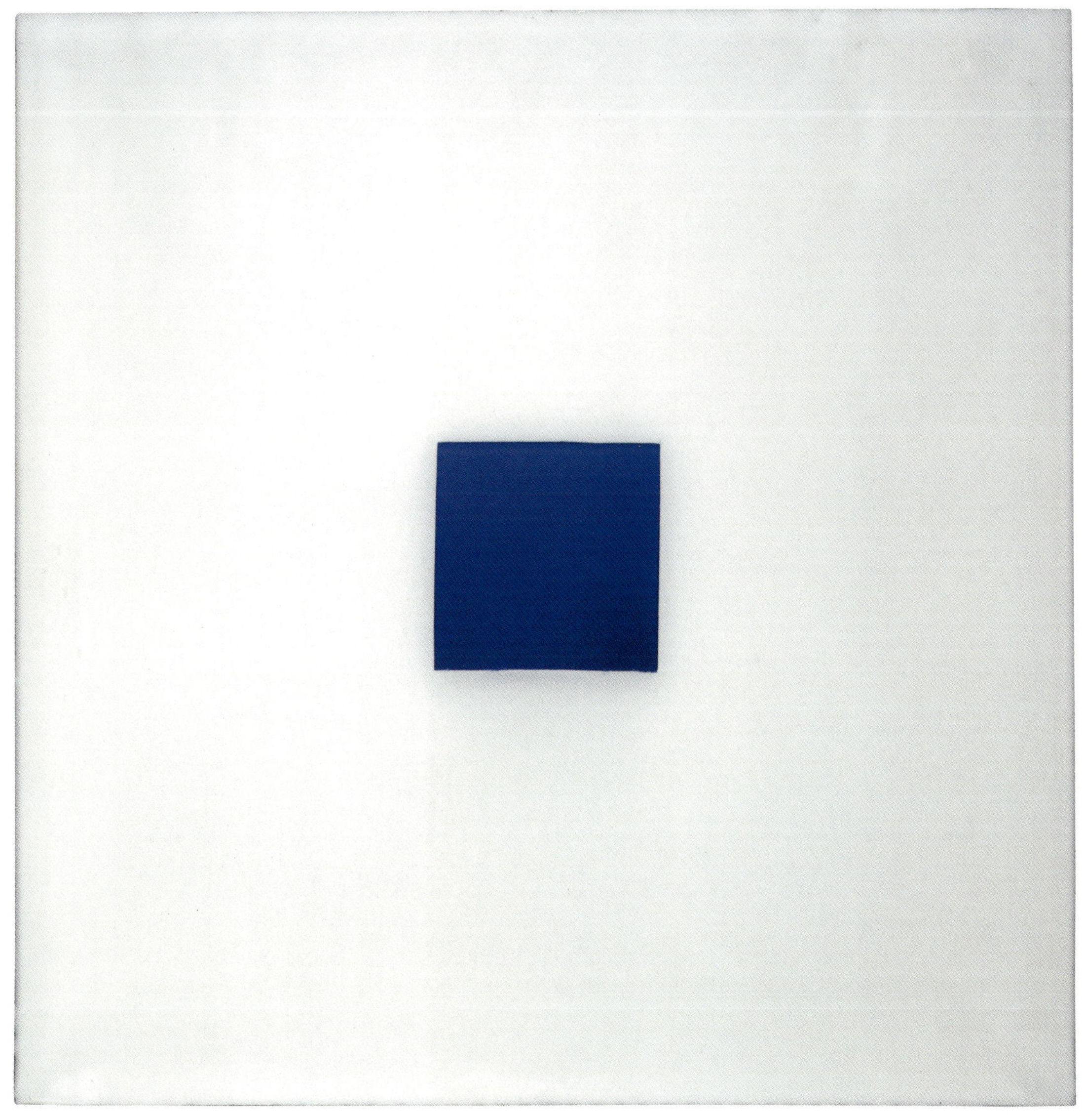

BIOGRAPHIES

AGNES MARTIN: Born in 1911 in Maklin, Saskatchewan, Canada, Agnes Martin immigrated to the United States at the age of nineteen. She attended Western Washington College of Education, Bellingham (1935–38); Teachers College, Columbia University, New York (1941–42 and 1951–52); and the University of New Mexico, Albuquerque (1946–47). Trained as a teacher, she taught art in both public schools and at universities. At the request of Betty Parsons, Martin left New Mexico and moved to New York (1957–67), where she befriended Ellsworth Kelly, Robert Indiana and James Rosenquist, among others. She abandoned both New York and painting in 1967, eventually settling again in New Mexico, where she resumed painting in the 1970s. Martin's art has been shown nationally and internationally on a continual basis since 1958. She was awarded the Alexej von Jawlensky Prize (1991) and the Oskar Kokoschka Prize (1992). The artist lives in Taos, New Mexico, where, at the age of ninety-two, she continues to paint every morning.

MARIA MARTINEZ: Born in circa 1887 in San Ildefonso Pueblo, New Mexico, Maria Martinez (née Maria Poveka Montoya) worked throughout her life in partnership with many members of her family. With her husband Julian, Martinez began making pottery in 1908 after being encouraged by Edgar L. Hewett, director of the School of American Research. Their early polychrome pottery shows their knowledge of earlier ceramic designs and forms. In 1912 they began making polished blackware for which they ultimately became renowned. In 1915 Maria and Julian Martinez participated in the Panama-California Exposition and in 1934 they were special exhibitors at the Chicago World's Fair Century of Progress. After the death of her husband in 1943, Martinez produced pottery in collaboration with her daughter-in-law, Santana Martinez (1943–56); her son, Popovi Da (1956–70); and her grandson, Tony E. Martinez (1967–68). She received numerous awards, including two honorary doctorates, one from Columbia College, Chicago, and another from the College of Santa Fe. Her long and productive career came to an end with her death in 1980.

FLORENCE PIERCE: Born in 1918 in Washington, D.C., Florence Pierce (née Florence Miller) began her art training at the Studio School of the Phillips Collection (1935–36). A few years later, Pierce moved to Taos, New Mexico, to study with Emil Bisttram, at his eponymously named school (1936–39). Subsequently, she joined his Transcendentalist Painting Group (1938–41). Pierce has worked in a wide range of media: stone, wood, oil, watercolor and, most recently, poured resin on mirrored plexiglass. Her work has been shown throughout the western part of the United States in both one-person and group exhibitions. In 2003 she was presented the Governor's Award for Excellence in the Arts. She remains extremely productive, showing new work at least yearly in Santa Fe.

EXHIBITION CHECKLIST

AGNES MARTIN

AGNES MARTIN
The Islands, I–XII
gesso, synthetic polymer and graphite on canvas
6′ x 6′, 1979
Courtesy of the Whitney Museum
of American Art, New York
Purchased with funds from The Sondra
and Charles Gilman, Jr. Foundation, Inc.
and Evelyn and Leonard A. Lauder

AGNES MARTIN
Untitled #6
acrylic and pencil on canvas
6′ x 6′, 1984
Courtesy of a Private Collection

MARIA MARTINEZ

MARIA MARTINEZ AND JULIAN MARTINEZ
Untitled, clay, 3.5″ x 6″, n.d.
Courtesy of the Millicent Rogers Museum of
Northern New Mexico

MARIA MARTINEZ AND JULIAN MARTINEZ
Untitled, clay, 3″ x 3″, n.d.
Courtesy of the Millicent Rogers Museum of
Northern New Mexico

MARIA MARTINEZ
Untitled, clay, 12″ x 12″, c. 1940
Courtesy of the Millicent Rogers Museum of
Northern New Mexico

Height precedes width.

MARIA MARTINEZ AND POPOVI DA
Untitled, clay, 12″ diameter, n.d.
Gift of Barbara Long,
Museum of Indian Arts & Culture/
Laboratory of Anthropology

MARIA MARTINEZ AND JULIAN MARTINEZ
Untitled, clay, 11″ diameter, n.d.
Bequest of Rick Dillingham,
Museum of Indian Arts & Culture/
Laboratory of Anthropology

MARIA MARTINEZ AND JULIAN MARTINEZ
Untitled, clay, 12″ diameter, n.d.
Bequest of Rick Dillingham,
Museum of Indian Arts & Culture/
Laboratory of Anthropology

MARIA MARTINEZ AND JULIAN MARTINEZ
Untitled, clay, 13.5″ diameter, n.d.
Gift of R. E. Hill, Museum of Indian Arts
& Culture/Laboratory of Anthropology

MARIA MARTINEZ AND SANTANA MARTINEZ
Untitled, clay, 5.25″ diameter, n.d.
Herman C. and Bina L. Ilfeld Collection in the
Museum of Indian Arts & Culture/
Laboratory of Anthropology

MARIA MARTINEZ AND JULIAN MARTINEZ
Untitled, clay, 7″ diameter, n.d.
Gift of Dr. Edgar L. Hewett.
Courtesy of John and Linda Comstock
and the Abigail Van Vleck Charitable Trust,
Museum of Indian Arts & Culture/
Laboratory of Anthropology

MARIA MARTINEZ AND JULIAN MARTINEZ
Untitled, clay, 7″ diameter, n.d.
Gift of Dr. Edgar L. Hewett,
Museum of Indian Arts & Culture/
Laboratory of Anthropology

MARIA MARTINEZ AND POPOVI DA
Untitled, clay, 13.75″ diameter, n.d.
Bequest of Rick Dillingham,
Museum of Indian Arts & Culture/
Laboratory of Anthropology

MARIA MARTINEZ AND JULIAN MARTINEZ
Untitled, clay, 12″ diameter, n.d.
Gift of R. E. Hill, Museum of Indian Arts
& Culture/Laboratory of Anthropology

MARIA MARTINEZ AND JULIAN MARTINEZ
Untitled, clay, 14.5″ diameter, n.d.
Herman C. and Bina L. Ilfeld Collection in the
Museum of Indian Arts & Culture/
Laboratory of Anthropology

MARIA MARTINEZ AND SANTANA MARTINEZ
Untitled, clay, 11.25″ diameter, n.d.
Francis H. and Patricia N. Harlow
Collection in the Museum of Indian Arts
& Culture/Laboratory of Anthropology

MARIA MARTINEZ AND JULIAN MARTINEZ
Untitled, clay, 10.5″ x 9″, n.d.
Museum Purchase, Museum of Indian Arts
& Culture/Laboratory of Anthropology

MARIA MARTINEZ AND JULIAN MARTINEZ
Untitled, clay, 10″ x 10″, n.d.
Museum Purchase, Museum of Indian Arts
& Culture/Laboratory of Anthropology

MARIA MARTINEZ AND JULIAN MARTINEZ
Untitled, clay, 5.5″ x 6.5″, n.d.
Herman C. and Bina L. Ilfeld Collection in the
Museum of Indian Arts & Culture/
Laboratory of Anthropology

MARIA MARTINEZ AND JULIAN MARTINEZ
Untitled, clay, 11.75″ x 8.25″, n.d.
Gift of Mrs. H. Kelvin Magill,
Museum of Indian Arts & Culture/
Laboratory of Anthropology

MARIA MARTINEZ AND SANTANA MARTINEZ
Untitled, clay, 11″ diameter, n.d.
Museum Purchase, Museum of Indian Arts
& Culture/Laboratory of Anthropology

MARIA MARTINEZ AND POPOVI DA
Untitled, clay, 5″ x 5.25″, n.d.
Gift of Barbara Long,
Museum of Indian Arts & Culture/
Laboratory of Anthropology

MARIA MARTINEZ AND JULIAN MARTINEZ
Untitled, clay, 2.75″ x 6.5″, n.d.
Gift of Mrs. Wesley Bradfield,
Museum of Indian Arts & Culture/
Laboratory of Anthropology

MARIA MARTINEZ AND JULIAN MARTINEZ
Untitled, clay, 11.9″ x 10.9″, 1929
Courtesy of the School of American Research

MARIA MARTINEZ AND JULIAN MARTINEZ
Untitled, clay, 9.9″ x 13.1″, 1915
Courtesy of the School of American Research

MARIA MARTINEZ
Untitled, clay, 5.9″ x 12.9″, 1967
Courtesy of the School of American Research

MARIA MARTINEZ
Untitled, clay, 14.5″ x 11.5″, 1934
Courtesy of the School of American Research

MARIA MARTINEZ
Untitled, clay, 14.6″ x 14.7″, 1923
Courtesy of the School of American Research

MARIA MARTINEZ AND JULIAN MARTINEZ
Untitled, clay, 12″ diameter, n.d.
Courtesy of the School of American Research

MARIA MARTINEZ
Untitled, clay, 5.9″ x 9.9″, 1926
Courtesy of the School of American Research

MARIA MARTINEZ
Untitled, clay, 4.7″ x 5.6″, 1967
Courtesy of the School of American Research

MARIA MARTINEZ
Untitled, clay, 4″ x 4.5″, c. 1956
Courtesy of Martha R. Clift

FLORENCE PIERCE

FLORENCE PIERCE
Untitled, number 229
resin on plexiglass, 24″ x 24″, 1997
Courtesy of Florence Pierce
and Charlotte Jackson Fine Art, Inc.

FLORENCE PIERCE
Untitled, number 230
resin on plexiglass, 24″ x 24″, 1997
Courtesy of Florence Pierce
and Charlotte Jackson Fine Art, Inc.

FLORENCE PIERCE
Untitled, number C35
resin on plexiglass, 24″ x 24″, 1994
Courtesy of Florence Pierce
and Charlotte Jackson Fine Art, Inc.

FLORENCE PIERCE
Untitled, number 73
resin on plexiglass, 24″ x 24″, 1995
Courtesy of Florence Pierce
and Charlotte Jackson Fine Art, Inc.

FLORENCE PIERCE
Untitled, number 124
resin on plexiglass, 16″ x 16″, 1993
Courtesy of Florence Pierce
and Charlotte Jackson Fine Art, Inc.

FLORENCE PIERCE
Untitled, number 114
resin on plexiglass, 16″ x 16″, 1995
Courtesy of Florence Pierce
and Charlotte Jackson Fine Art, Inc.

FLORENCE PIERCE
Untitled, number 280,
resin on plexiglass, 16″ x 16″, 1998
Courtesy of Florence Pierce
and Charlotte Jackson Fine Art, Inc.

FLORENCE PIERCE
Untitled, number 112
resin on plexiglass, 16″ x 16″, 1993
Courtesy of Florence Pierce
and Charlotte Jackson Fine Art, Inc.

FLORENCE PIERCE
Untitled, number 89
resin on plexiglass, 16″ x 16″, 1993
Courtesy of Florence Pierce
and Charlotte Jackson Fine Art, Inc.

FLORENCE PIERCE
Untitled, number 280A
resin on plexiglass, 16″ x16″, 1998
Courtesy of Florence Pierce
and Charlotte Jackson Fine Art, Inc.

FLORENCE PIERCE
Untitled, number 81
resin on plexiglass, 16″ x 16″, 1992
Courtesy of Florence Pierce
and Charlotte Jackson Fine Art, Inc.

FLORENCE PIERCE
Untitled, number 2
resin on plexiglass, 16″ x 16″, n.d.
Courtesy of Florence Pierce
and Charlotte Jackson Fine Art, Inc.

FLORENCE PIERCE
Untitled, number 8
resin on plexiglass, 16″ x 16″, 1990
Courtesy of Florence Pierce
and Charlotte Jackson Fine Art, Inc.

FLORENCE PIERCE
Untitled, number 280
resin on plexiglass, 16″ x 16″, 1998
Courtesy of Florence Pierce
and Charlotte Jackson Fine Art, Inc.

FLORENCE PIERCE
Untitled, number 116
resin on plexiglass, 16″ x 16″, 1993
Courtesy of Florence Pierce
and Charlotte Jackson Fine Art, Inc.

FLORENCE PIERCE
Untitled, number 128
resin on plexiglass, 16″ x 16″, 1996
Courtesy of Florence Pierce
and Charlotte Jackson Fine Art, Inc.

FLORENCE PIERCE
Untitled, number 107
resin on plexiglass, 40″ x 40″, 1994
Courtesy of Florence Pierce
and Charlotte Jackson Fine Art, Inc.

FLORENCE PIERCE
Untitled, number 100A
resin on plexiglass, 40″ x 40″, 1994
Courtesy of Florence Pierce
and Charlotte Jackson Fine Art, Inc.

FLORENCE PIERCE
Untitled, number 108
resin on plexiglass, 40″ x 40″, 1994
Courtesy of Ellen Berkman

FLORENCE PIERCE
Untitled, number 106
resin on plexiglass, 40″ x 40″, 1994
Courtesy of Florence Pierce
and Charlotte Jackson Fine Art, Inc.

FLORENCE PIERCE
Untitled, number 105
resin on plexiglass, 40″ x 40″, 1994
Courtesy of Florence Pierce
and Charlotte Jackson Fine Art, Inc.

FLORENCE PIERCE
Untitled, number 104
resin on plexiglass, 40″ x 40″, 1994
Courtesy of Florence Pierce
and Charlotte Jackson Fine Art, Inc.

FLORENCE PIERCE
Untitled, number 101
resin on plexiglass, 40″ x 40″, 1994
Courtesy of Florence Pierce
and Charlotte Jackson Fine Art, Inc.

FLORENCE PIERCE
Untitled, number 102
resin on plexiglass, 40″ x 40″, 1994
Courtesy of Florence Pierce
and Charlotte Jackson Fine Art, Inc.

FLORENCE PIERCE
Untitled, number 67
resin on plexiglass, 16″ x 16″, 1992
Courtesy of Mr. Thomas P. Lang, Jr.

FLORENCE PIERCE
Untitled, number 271
resin on plexiglass, 16″ x 16″, 1998
Courtesy of Florence Pierce
and Charlotte Jackson Fine Art, Inc.

FLORENCE PIERCE
Untitled, number 47
resin on plexiglass, 24″ x 24″, 1994
Courtesy of Florence Pierce
and Charlotte Jackson Fine Art, Inc.

FLORENCE PIERCE
Untitled, number 190
resin on plexiglass, 24″ x 24″, 1996
Courtesy of Florence Pierce
and Charlotte Jackson Fine Art, Inc.

FLORENCE PIERCE
Untitled, number 87
resin on plexiglass 24″ x 24″, 1993
Courtesy of Florence Pierce
and Charlotte Jackson Fine Art, Inc.

ACKNOWLEDGMENTS

Exhibitions should always be subtitled collaborations. I have been fortunate to work with many talented people who all contributed to this project. Governor Bill Richardson and First Lady Barbara Richardson created the opportunity for me to undertake this exhibit and my gratitude will long outlive this project. Former New Mexico Representative J. Paul Taylor served as a champion of this endeavor and his gentle persuasion of the state legislators to fund this project showed the grace and sensitivity for which he has long been praised. Others who helped guide this undertaking through the political process that I particularly wish to thank are: Lee Witt, Eric Witt, Anne Green Romig and, most importantly, Stuart Ashman, Secretary of the Department of Cultural Affairs. I hope I have had enough good manners to thank throughout this project the indispensable staff at the Museum of Fine Arts and its sister institutions. Their daily support allowed this endeavor to be better than I could have envisioned. Particularly deserving of continued gratitude are: Blair Clark, Theresa Garcia, Mary Jebsen, Anita McNeece, Velma Rodriguez and Joan Tafoya. Outside of our state institutions, Charlotte Jackson and Sarah Deats of Charlotte Jackson Fine Arts, Inc., must be mentioned first because they have been steadfast supporters, tireless workers and good friends. Similarly, Edward Holgate has steadily guided this project from conception to completion. His assistance truly made this project viable. Oliver Chambers, Bob Ellis, Thomas P. Lang Jr., Jeff Mahan, General Manager, The Anasazi Restaurant, Barbara and Michael Ogg, Terry Rodgers and Sean Ulmer offered only good advice and assistance at crucial moments in this project. The staffs at Pace Gallery, the Millicent Rogers Museum of Northern New Mexico, the School of American Research and the Whitney Museum of American Art gave me only pleasure and assistance during the creation of this exhibition. My immediate collaborators, designers Susan Hyde-Holmes, David Mendez and John Tinker; editor Laura Addison; and co-writers Marsha C. Bol and Lucy Lippard contributed their intelligence, creativity and support without ever demanding anything in return. Such generosity deserves recognition. Finally, my deepest appreciation goes to the most vital participants in this undertaking, the artists, Agnes Martin, Maria Martinez and Florence Pierce, who offer all of us the gift of their art. In so doing, they allow us to collaborate with them as they forge their paths to perfection.

DEPARTMENT OF CULTURAL AFFAIRS
Stuart A. Ashman, *Secretary*
Bergit Salazar, *Deputy Secretary*

MUSEUM OF FINE ARTS
Marsha C. Bol, Ph.D., *Director*
Mary Jebsen, *Assistant Director*
Tim Rodgers, Ph.D., *Chief Curator*
Laura Addison, *Curator of Contemporary Art*
Arif Khan, *Curator of the Governor's Gallery*
Christine Mather, *Curator of Collections*
Joseph Traugott, Ph.D., *Curator of 20th-Century Art*
Steve Yates, *Curator of Photography*
Ellen Zieselman, *Curator of Education*
Michael Abatemarco, *Sergeant of Security*
Theresa Garcia, *Administrator/Financial Specialist*
Martha Landry, *Special Events Coordinator*
Dominic Martinez, *Captain of Security*
Velma Rodriguez, *Secretary*
Charles Sloan, *Chief Preparator*
Joan Tafoya, *Registrar*

WE HAVE TO HAVE
PATIENCE FOR
EVERYTHING...
GO AHEAD
AND WORK SLOWLY.

—MARIA MARTINEZ

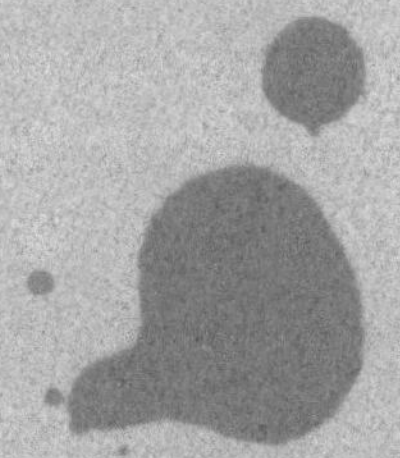

WE HAVE TO HAVE PATIENCE FOR EVERYTHING... GO AHEAD AND WORK SLOWLY.

MARIA MARTINS

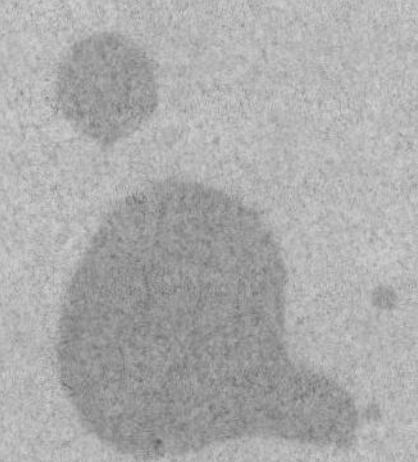